Fiona Harrold's earliest exposure to coaching was at the age of 11 when, as she was growing up in Northern Ireland, her beloved father would inspire her with the works of Norman Vincent Peale, Napoleon Hill and Dale Carnegie.

Fiona's intention is to take the principles of personal responsibility, individual self-help and mutual support to the widest public through her books, workshops and website services. She is the author of the bestselling *Be Your Own Life Coach*, *The 10-Minute Life Coach*, *Reinvent Yourself* and *Indestructible Self-Belief*. She was recently named by *The Times* as one of the 'new gurus who have got inside our minds to fill society's spiritual void'.

Fiona was the Green Party Parliamentary candidate for Hammersmith and Fulham at the 2005 general election. She lives in London with her teenage son.

Also by Fiona Harrold and available from Hodder Mobius

Be Your Own Life Coach
The 10-Minute Life Coach

Fiona Harrold

The 7 Rules of Success

Follow the Strategies, Experience the Results

First published in Great Britain in 2006 by Hodder & Stoughton
A division of Hodder Headline

A Mobius paperback

1

A CIP catalogue record for this title is available from the British Library

ISBN 978 0 340 83204 2
ISBN 0 340 83204 5

Typeset in Sabon MT by Palimpsest Book Production Limited,
Polmont, Stirlingshire

Printed and bound by
Mackays of Chatham Ltd, Chatham, Kent

Hodder Headline's policy is to use papers that are natural,
renewable and recyclable products and made from
wood grown in sustainable forests. The logging and
manufacturing processes are expected to conform to the
environmental regulations of the country of origin.

Hodder & Stoughton Ltd
A division of Hodder Headline
338 Euston Road
London NW1 3BH

DEDICATION

For all of you brave people determined to make a success of your lives, for your own good and the good of everyone. I admire and salute you!

And for the many readers of *Be Your Own Life Coach* and *The 10-Minute Life Coach* who have taken the time to write and tell me of your successes. Thank you for your generosity; you have inspired me and kept me motivated. More success to you!

> This is the true joy in life, being used for a purpose recognised by yourself as a mighty one, being a true force of Nature instead of a feverish little clod of ailments and grievances complaining that the world will not devote itself to making you happy . . . I want to be thoroughly used up when I die. For the harder I work, the more I live. I rejoice in life for its own sake. Life is no brief candle for me. It's a sort of splendid torch which I've got to hold up for the moment and I want to make it burn as brightly as possible before handing it on to future generations.
>
> George Bernard Shaw

CONTENTS

Welcome to *The 7 Rules of Success* 1
1: Be Passionate 9
2: Practise Self-belief 43
3: Do More! 79
4: Take More Risks 106
5: Inspire Others 142
6: Persevere 176
7: Be Generous 211
And Finally . . . 245

ACKNOWLEDGEMENTS

This book would not have been possible but for the time and generosity given by everyone interviewed. I thank you all for that.

Thanks also to my great pal Rita Hamill for arranging all the meetings and conversations and to Rose Smith and Catherine Lee Smith for their painstaking transcribing of those hours and hours of tapes.

Finally, thanks so much to everyone at Hodder Mobius for their enthusiasm and support for this project: in particular, Rowena Webb, for sticking by me through shifting deadlines over three years and the formidable and brilliant editor that is Helen Coyle, who was always right! Thanks, laydees.

Welcome TO THE 7 RULES OF SUCCESS

I have been thinking about success, about what it means and how you achieve it, for the last three years. During that time I have talked to the successful people whose stories appear in this book about how they do what they do.

I wanted to take the mystery out of success, to lay bare the thinking behind great achievement, and to expose the strategies and secrets of outstanding individuals. This is the core of *The 7 Rules of Success*. In the process I have been able to identify the 7 Rules that great modern achievers follow, the ones that you too can use to transform your life. All the achievers in this book follow all these rules, but I have selected four people for each rule who demonstrate it most forcefully.

Use this book as your success manual, your rulebook. If you apply the thinking, follow the strategies and adopt the behaviour suggested, you will experience the results. I believe that what you read here will prove invaluable to you in your quest for success, whatever that means to you, whatever age you are, in your journey through life. All you need to get started is a notebook to jot down responses to the questions I'm going to be asking you to answer – and an appetite for success.

The Meaning of Success

Earlier success guides have really just conflated success with having lots of money. The success they focused on was overwhelmingly material, a rags-to-riches guide. Given the times they were written in, this was entirely appropriate as their authors had often pulled themselves out of terrible poverty to achieve great wealth. They came mainly from the United States in the 1930s in the aftermath of the Great Depression and the years following the Second World War. Napoleon Hill's *Think and Grow Rich* (1937) and Dale Carnegie's *How to Win Friends and Influence People* (1936), surely the bible for salesmen everywhere, sold in their millions. Then came Norman Vincent Peale's *The Power of Positive Thinking* (1952), and W. Clement Stone's *Success Through a Positive Mental Attitude* (1960). All are classic self-help guides, written for a generation raised on the American Dream of freedom through affluence.

Nowadays, we in the developed world enjoy greater prosperity and comfort than our forefathers could ever have imagined. We work fewer hours; we have more disposable income; we're better educated and we are cushioned by a social welfare system that supports us from cradle to grave. We have really never had it so good. We should be the happiest generation in history. Yet we are not.

Happiness and Success

Depending on which study you look at, we are less happy than we were fifty years ago. Why is it that happiness levels have not risen in the past half-century, despite massive increases in personal and state wealth? Research suggests that once people reach an 'adequate' income, additional wealth rarely has any further positive effect on happiness or satisfaction. Even economists are pointing out that economic growth and prosperity cannot be read as indicators of happiness. This is what Andrew Oswald, Professor of Economics at Warwick University, said in May 2004:

> The improvement in prosperity over the last thirty years has had no effect on reported levels of life satisfaction or happiness in the UK and that is quite remarkable. This is a serious challenge for policy makers as it appears to be very difficult to make people happy in the Western world.

Wealth has increased much faster than happiness partly because governments have striven to increase people's spending power rather than taking a broader view of what makes them feel good. Richard Layard, a leading British economist and long-standing advisor to the Labour Government, has just published a book that asks: 'What is the point of economic policy if not to make us generally happier?' In *Happiness: Lessons from a New Science* he calls for a radical revision of public policy and suggests an emphasis away from wealth creation to happiness as the ultimate goal.

Our definition of what makes for a successful life is undergoing a re-evaluation. We are questioning the value of affluence achieved at the cost of our health and a shortened lifespan; or a working life so demanding that we neglect our children and feel drained of energy and joy. We are suspicious of an economic prosperity that may be unsustainable and destroys much of the planet for our children. We are increasingly uncomfortable with a lifestyle that relies on child labour and sweatshops in poorer countries.

We have come to prize time over money, knowing it's the one thing we can never get back once it's gone. We are beginning to reaffirm the importance of personal relationships and many of us long for a less driven, more relaxed way of life. I believe that there has been a fundamental shift in our attitude to success. It has been coming for a while and now its moment has truly arrived.

We are seeking fulfilment. We want a life less mundane and materialistic: more meaningful and significant. We want to choose our own fate, determine our own destiny, without restriction. Our post-war affluence has made us ambitious. More of us are better educated than ever before, our horizons extended, our aspirations limitless. Easy travel has made the planet a smaller place, widening our perspective, exposing us to other worlds and ways of life. Some will say this is the reason we are less content, more restless than our forefathers of fifty years ago. I say it's the challenge of freedom and opportunity. This can be either a burden or a gift.

We are no longer willing merely to make a living, however lucrative. We are not content to do a job just so that later we'll be able to afford to please ourselves. All of us are taking a close look inside to see what it is that we really want. And we live with the contemporary notion of personal responsibility: that the direction of our lives is down to us. We can create our own results. We don't have to live the life we were born into, or the one we were schooled to follow. Life really is what you make it.

Modern psychology has taught us that we choose how we think. In the past, experts believed that we were pre-programmed in our early years and had little control over our thinking. Not any more. The good news is that we can choose to think that we are in charge of our destiny and alter our behaviour accordingly. We can decide to ramp-up our thinking to become more pro-active, enterprising, resourceful and dynamic.

Living an ideal life, based on our definition of success, is the name of the game. And the greatest stumbling block to accomplishing our dreams is always within.

Success Is Personal

Success is what you make it mean. It can also change over time. I am regularly confronted by wealthy individuals who enjoy all the status and trappings that come from being at the top of their professional tree, yet feel like losers. Why? Because they are leading a life that matches their parents' dreams and aspirations, not one that feels right or fulfilling to them. Or because, unlike their peers who are prepared to put up with another five years of relentless work to achieve partnership and further prestige, they realise they cannot carry on faking commitment. Success nowadays is more personal than for any other generation. The trick is to figure out what success looks like to you and go after it. Keeping up with the neighbours is over.

More and more people are leaving highly-paid jobs to 'downshift' to a less frenetic way of life. Downshifting has become more than a dream for millions of people across the richest countries. Research by Datamonitor, the market analysts, estimates that 2.6 million Britons are downshifters, compared with 1.7 million in 1997 when, according to Polly Ghazi and Judy Jones in their book *Downshifting*, the 'quiet revolt against the culture of getting and spending' began. The movement is so well established that Datamonitor predicts we will have 3.7 million downshifters by 2007, part of a movement of 12 million people throughout Europe. Locked into the cycle of earning more in order to spend more seems increasingly meaningless to millions. In the US, downshifting is said to have the potential to bring about the most fundamental change in lifestyles since the Depression of the early 1930s. Whereas, previously, standards of living were assumed to be directly linked to quality of life, now people are actually choosing to earn less in order to do something more rewarding, or simply to have more time.

Success and Status

Modern success also means you can take jobs that were previously considered low-status, without losing status! Training colleges offering plumbing courses are being flooded with applications –

many from graduates with good degrees, looking for a career change. Recently, at Leicester College, there were around four hundred applications for twenty places on the full-time NVQ plumbing course, while Hackney Community College in London received eight hundred applications for just thirty-five places on their four-year course. Some of the applicants had held jobs as accountants, stockbrokers or historians. Hackney College's head of plumbing, Ken Daniels, said, 'I'm not surprised people are switching from white-collar jobs. They see plumbing as a bit more creative and stress-free and relaxing . . . they are also more in control of their own destiny if they're going to be self-employed.' Success has never been more meritocratic.

Doing What You Love Is Still the Key

Success guides then and now are united in emphasising one rule above all others. That rule is to do what you love doing. Over sixty years ago Dale Carnegie said, 'You never achieve success unless you like what you are doing.' I agree, and so does every person I spoke to in researching this book. Regardless of the nature of their success, loving what they did was at the heart of everyone's story. You'll find this discussed in detail in Rule 1: **Be Passionate.** When your heart isn't in something, it's hard to do it well. Motivation, enthusiasm, energy and inspiration will all slump and you will never produce the results that you're capable of. You'll infect everyone around you and pull everything down, including the bottom line. This applies in particular to the work area of your life, but is true for any activity you engage in.

The belief that dreams are impossible to achieve prevents most people from getting what they want out of life. In fact, each one of us needs to check our thinking regularly for traces of restriction or resignation. To stay fully alive we need to remain alert to our passion to ensure that we still love what we do.

Modern life means we can change direction and do something different with the next five years than we did with the last five. And the big advantage of staying awake to your passion is that you need never have a mid-life crisis, at any age!

The New Rules of Success

We need different rules for different times. We live in a different world from our parents and grandparents. Some of the rules you'll find here fit with the spirit of our age, the cultural zeitgeist. They apply to our current life and times and would not have been so relevant a generation ago. For example, Rule 7: **Be Generous** takes into account our shift in thinking on what makes for a successful business. The ethics of a company now come under far greater scrutiny than ever before. Consumers can influence the profitability of a company by boycotting its products and services, or can even help to close it if they find its practices and policies distasteful.

The fifth rule, **Inspire Others**, reflects a more co-operative way of working as distinct from the old 'them and us' approach. Nowadays we want to feel included and a valued member of our organisation, and not just an employee. We want to be part of a winning team that's doing something worthwhile. Our reward is a deeper satisfaction than a wage slip can offer. A successful venture or business must be able to inspire its supporters, members or employees to hold on to them and flourish.

So What Do Successful People Look Like Now?

A successful person isn't simply one who is a millionaire by the age of 25, though that's fine too, as you'll see with Joe Dhinsa. Among the people I spoke to in the course of my research was Carmel McConnell who gave up a lucrative career to provide breakfast for inner-city schoolchildren, through her charity, the Magic Breakfast. Another way to think of success is to imagine someone having a bright idea and the guts to make it work and provide employment for others, as Tamara Hill-Norton has done with her Sweaty Betty chain of women's sportswear shops. Then there's Christina Noble, the mother who has saved the lives of thousands of Vietnamese street children. Success might mean living on less than £8,000 a year so that you are free to campaign against human rights abuses, as Peter Tatchell does. It could entail giving up a high-flying City career to follow your dream of having a flower shop, as Kally Ellis did. It means never giving up on yourself so that your umpteenth bright idea can still happen later in life, as with Simon Woodroffe and his brilliant Yo! Sushi restaurants. There again, a successful person might be someone like Chris Sade, who arrived in London at the age of 16 not knowing anyone and not speaking much English, took a job washing dishes and ended up on the board of the same company in his early thirties.

Success Is What Success Means to You

Over the pages that follow you'll have time to discover and clarify what exactly success looks like to you. You'll hear the wisdom and benefit from the experiences of fabulous individuals who, like me, are committed to your success. Listen to their stories and learn from their insights, experiences and achievements.

While searching for inner truth, you'll also find brilliant tips and practical information – whether you want to fine-tune your life or get a brand-new one.

Let's go!

1: *Be* PASSIONATE

Passion is the driving force behind every significant human achievement, from discovering the light bulb to defeating Hitler. A successful life has to be underpinned by passion, otherwise you are building your life on shaky foundations, which may well require restructuring later on. Some of the most unfulfilled and frustrated people I've ever come across have had everything money can buy but there's still something missing. It's called passion.

I'm not suggesting that we can ignore money. Clearly, providing for ourselves is an intrinsic part of a successful life and, as my brother Brian is wont to point out, it certainly helps when you go to the shops! However, in the hunt for happiness, money alone is not the answer. Study after study shows record levels of dissatisfaction with modern life. Young people, in particular, enjoying the highest living standards since records began, are often deeply miserable during the proverbial 'best years of their lives'. Two-thirds of Britons aged between 18 and 35 feel depressed or unhappy, according to a major survey carried out a few years ago by analysts Publicis.

Another recently published study reports that eight out of ten young high-flyers in Britain are suffering a 'quarter-life crisis'. They feel disillusioned by their jobs and are re-evaluating what they want from life. Ninety per cent of those questioned

– men and women aged 25 to 35 – are seeking careers which would add purpose to their lives. Julia Middleton, chief executive of Common Purpose, the leadership development organisation which commissioned the report, said: 'Emerging leaders want to make a good living, but they also want to make a difference . . . They will not stay with employers who do not support their efforts to find purpose in their lives . . . In an attempt to satisfy their longing to make a difference, they often drop out of their fast track or job-hop.'

There's just no mistaking this change in our outlook. We want more out of life, and money can't buy it. I believe that the key thing most of us are missing is passion.

To Be Happy, You Need to Be Passionate

A happy life is what we're all after. What's the secret? Is there a formula? One man who has spent thirty years and $30 million researching these questions is Martin Seligman, a psychologist at the University of Pennsylvania. He has worked out what he sees as a blueprint for happiness. He believes there are three routes to happiness, which he calls the 'pleasant life', the 'good life' and the 'meaningful life'. The pleasant life sees superficial pleasures as the key to happiness, and it is this that many people mistakenly pursue. 'The biggest mistake that people in the rich West make is to be enchanted with the Hollywood idea of happiness, which is really just giggling and smiling a lot,' Seligman says. While a life bent on instant pleasure and gratification offers some degree of happiness, it is ultimately unsatisfying on its own.

Seligman believes that money isn't the answer either. He reports that once we have enough to pay for life's essentials such as food and a roof over our heads, more money adds little to our happiness.

To be seriously happy, Seligman says, we have to aim for the good life and the meaningful life. And here is the formula. You have to identify what he terms your 'signature strengths', your intrinsic talents and strengths, which could be anything from perseverance and leadership to an ability to entertain others. Using those strengths in our working and social life will help us achieve what he calls a good life.

But the most underrated of all, according to Seligman, is the meaningful life – devoting oneself to an institution or cause greater than oneself. In a now classic exercise Seligman calls 'Philanthropy versus Fun', psychology students in one of his classes undertook to engage in one pleasurable activity and one philanthropic activity, and write about both. The results, he claims, were 'life-changing'. The afterglow of the fun activity (watching a film, eating ice cream) paled in comparison with the effects of the kind action (volunteering to work in a soup kitchen, helping at the school fair). The reason, Seligman suggests, is that kindness is a gratification. 'It calls on your strengths to rise to an occasion and meet a challenge. Kindness . . . consists in total engagement and in the loss of self-consciousness.'

What Should I Do with My Life?

A sense of purpose brings passion into your life. It gives it meaning and you'll avoid the quarter-life, mid-life or any other life crisis. The only good thing about a crisis is that at least it might get you thinking, but how much better to be aware of your purpose and be passionate about it without the angst! Aligning your purpose with your signature strengths is the surefire route to personal fulfilment and a successful life. Knowing that you're living out your potential and fullest expression of yourself puts you in very good company as well. A sense of purpose is at the very top of the pyramid of personal fulfilment created by Abraham Maslow more than fifty years ago. Through his research, Dr Maslow discovered that those who feel purposeful are expressing the highest qualities that humanity has to offer.

The question 'What should I do with my life?' is at the heart of all our lives, one that I come across most frequently in talks and workshops. Often, people have been so driven or drained by the sheer pace of their lives that this is their only opportunity to think it through. They are caught up in the 'too busy earning a living to get a life' dilemma.

An enforced retreat from one's life can provide the time for reflection that one is looking for. While it may not be your first choice, a prison sentence can give you that time out that you have failed to give yourself! I received a letter recently from James, 41, who is serving a four-year sentence for insider share dealing and whose enforced thinking time was proving invaluable. Life on the outside had been frantic as he had built up a successful career in property and finance, married and had two children. His career success had given him a tremendous standard of living.

When I heard from James, he was clear that he had committed a crime, was paying the price and was determined to put that time out to the best possible use. He was reading every motivational and self-help book ever written, and was taking an Open University degree in psychology. He had begun to coach his fellow inmates, using my first book, *Be Your Own Life Coach*, and was discovering a genuine talent for motivating and inspiring others to take responsibility and get to grips with their lives. He was encouraging men who had been imprisoned for fifteen years to take training courses and helping them figure out how they were going to 'go straight' after their release.

Intrigued, I went to visit him and saw that he had become the resident coach for the entire prison. New prisoners were directed to his cell so that he could influence them from the outset, while those nearing their release date worked intensively with him to plan their new lives. James explained how the United Kingdom has some of the worst re-offending rates in the world and that only the sort of personal coaching he was offering could change this. His vision was to work with me to bring this about and, in doing so, reduce the re-offending and crime rate throughout the country. The benefit to all of us is obvious. James was a superb example of someone using their strengths and talents to the full to achieve something meaningful, living a purpose-driven life. He was one of the best motivated and most passionate individuals I had ever met. And far happier and fulfilled than many, many people on the 'outside'.

How ironic it is that in workshops I have often asked people what they would do if they were locked up in prison! It's a great question to get you focused on what's really important to you and what your signature strengths are. In a moment, I'll talk you through an exercise to clarify your passion and purpose, but first I want to introduce you to the wonderful Kally Ellis.

Kally is the founder of top London florists, McQueen's, a favourite of Gwyneth Paltrow and Elton John and patronised by shops like Gucci, Hermès, Bulgari and Cartier. For ten years she has been the florist at the most glamorous event in the world, the *Vanity Fair* post-Oscars party in Hollywood. Along with her business partner, Ercole Moroni, she runs two shops and a floristry school, and is poised to open a lifestyle retreat in Italy. She began her career working in a French bank in London's financial district. Losing her best friend in the Lockerbie air disaster of 1988 made her re-evaluate her life.

Kally Ellis

I woke up one morning having had this incredibly vivid dream. Looking down a tunnel I could see nothing but a flower shop. The dream – it felt like a vision, really – came as a thunderbolt. I woke determined to resign from the job I loathed and set up a flower shop. I found myself thinking, 'Yes, that's it. You've got to run your own flower business.' I had no experience or relevant business skills but spent the next three months learning floral skills, while I still worked at the bank. I did freelance work for no pay at local florists at weekends, and on one of those jobs – to decorate a Christmas tree – met my business partner, Ercole Moroni. It then took me three months to find that first shop.

I thought, 'It's now or never. I've got to do this.' I was 27 when I started McQueen's. It never crossed my mind that it was going to fail. The weirdest thing is that I didn't even have a passion for flowers when I was growing up. But years ago in Paris, I was completely mesmerised at how a tiny, local florist could hand-tie a bouquet from a simple bunch of tulips. In those days, that was unheard-of in Britain. I was bowled over by this and was sure so many others would be too. People didn't realise how much more beautiful things can look. If you don't show them, then they don't know it's there.

When we opened our first shop in Shoreditch, east London, on 1 January 1991, it was the height of the recession and flowers were a luxury item. Analyst friends of mine in the City warned me against it. But there was a complete burning desire inside me to do it. So I stormed ahead like a bull in a china shop and I think it was purely my ignorance of not really knowing what was ahead that pulled me through. If I had done loads of research I would never have done it. It's kind of scary looking back. Some of those friends in the City have subsequently been made redundant.

My business partner is fantastic. Although Ercole is completely dyslexic, phone phobic and unable to deal with people unless he's face-to-face with them, he is incredibly creative and I learnt so much from him. Our window displays were spectacular. Lots of people would get a glimpse as they went by in their cars, or on the bus, so we got a lot of phone calls. The entire business was built on word of mouth.

Mind you, in the beginning it was touch-and-go. We took over a plant landscaping business that had a small flower annexe but no passing trade due to one of the first red routes in London being painted right outside our door! We even took on its name: McQueen's. Looking back, it was an incredibly stupid thing to do. I had £14,000 in savings to invest but inherited a £40,000 debt from an unknown East End florists, who clearly didn't have a clue. They'd even fallen out with the flower market due to their bouncing cheques. By the end of the first year, our debts were paid off and we were showing a small profit. We simplified the whole approach to floristry, creating a contemporary, minimal but clean look, which appealed. We revealed the simplicity and beauty of one type of flower and how it could be displayed. And our reputation led on to more and more press interest, culminating in a recent one-hour television documentary programme called Celebrity Florists.

The success has entailed working from the early hours of the morning until late at night. It is a big commitment with a young family and you have to put the time in. But my passion has always kept me moving forward, never looking back and never standing still. I am always on the move, always looking for that next thing. And so, McQueen's grew very rapidly. There are now twenty-five of us.

I always say yes. I've never ever thrown business away. If I can hold on to it, I will. Ten years ago I helped someone out and it paid off. Vanity Fair *magazine had flown a celebrity French florist over to do the flowers for their Oscars party at the Serpentine Gallery in London. This was to be a VIP dinner-dance with A-list guests. The guest of honour was Diana, Princess of Wales (in that black dress, remember?). The florist only brought over two helpers when the event required a team of twenty and he didn't even know where the flower market was. Through a convoluted chain of events, we were asked if we could save the day. I remember thinking, Am I ready for this? I've never done anything on this scale before. But then I just thought, Actually, yes, I am.*

So, we got loads of freelancers on board, worked around the clock and the organiser was delighted with the result. It's now our tenth year of doing the Vanity Fair Oscars party flowers. This has led on to the Cannes Film Festival every year, the new Tribeca Film Festival in New York, and next year we do the Venice Biennial.

I wake up every day and I love going to work. I'm one of those very few lucky people I know who absolutely adores what I do. It's not about the money, or the success. It's because I love working with flowers and I love the pleasure it gives people. I love taking flowers home to my mum at the end of the week. It's just fantastic.

Kally's story reads like a fairy tale. Yet, one of the things that impressed me most about her when we met was her focus, drive and unrelenting appetite for hard work. Driven by the dream, she was none the less entirely realistic about making the business work, with no romantic notions that success would magically materialise. She demonstrates forcefully the winning combination of passion coupled with dynamic action. Passion and having a vision for your life is vital for driving your life forwards. Harnessing that passion to relentless action is key. Observe how Kally paid attention to her dream. Whether you see it as divine intervention or her own inner wisdom, what's interesting is that she took it seriously and acted on the feeling it gave her. How often do people ignore this inner guidance, suppress the yearning and forget the dream? How often do they dismiss their desires as impossible and unrealistic? Settling for what's safe and feels secure may provide some comfort, but it could also rob you of your dreams and *joie de vivre*. As George Bernard Shaw wrote:

> **The reasonable man adapts himself to the conditions that surround him. The unreasonable man adapts surrounding conditions to himself. All progress depends on the unreasonable man.**

On paper, Kally's plan to leave a well-paid, secure job to set up a florist was entirely 'unreasonable', yet by staying true to her passion and, at the same time, being pragmatic and practical, she gave herself every chance of success.

Be realistic about passion. Sometimes I come across people who expect passion to give them a continual buzz, to be on a constant high, and are disappointed that everyday life can sometimes feel so ordinary. They search endlessly for the next big thing, feeling that their real passion is just around the corner. The thrill of passion may drive you in a particular direction, but the day-to-day reality of doing the work is often and unavoidably more mundane. I was a parliamentary candidate at the last general election and, however passionate I may be about green politics, handing out leaflets outside tube stations is pretty tedious. However, it was all part of the job of saving the planet and had to be done. Ensure that you're realistic about the workaday expression of your conviction.

Passion and Purpose

You need a sense of purpose to bring passion into your life. Look at anyone who lives life passionately and you'll find a sense of purpose underpinning their approach to life. You too have always had a purpose, whether declared or undeclared, hidden or revealed. Frequently, people are alerted to their purpose after a major shock, illness or bereavement, a wake-up call, if you like. I have even met people who have suffered a knock on the head, through an accident, that has triggered them to think about the purpose of their life. But there's no need to wait for outside intervention. Divining your own sense of purpose is your prerogative at any time you like. One thing is for sure. Having that sense of purpose within you will lend more power to all that you do.

Take the wildly successful double act, Susannah and Trinny, the stylists who have their own TV show and have written best-selling books. Watching them on television for the first time, I could see that they genuinely cared about the clothes their 'victims' were choosing. Defending their straight-talking approach, Trinny said, 'We never feel that we are being cutting about people. We don't say things for effect: it's what we believe. Everything comes from our passionate desire to help women make the best of themselves. If you look good, sex is better, your self-esteem is better, your life is better.' They can see the potential in anyone to look great and are aware of the overall benefit this will bring to people's lives. They get a huge buzz from it as well.

What's Your Vision?

Answer these simple questions with five words or a short statement for each:

1. What do you want most out of life?
   e.g. to be happy and feel fulfilled

2. What do you want to see happen in the world?
   e.g. peace and happiness

3. What makes you special?
   e.g. my energy, drive and enthusiasm, ability to inspire and motivate others

4. What things can you do/are you capable of doing right now?
   e.g. writing, public speaking, coaching

Now write this statement as follows:
I will . . . (*choose one answer from 4*), using my . . . (*answer from 3*), *to accomplish* . . . (answer from 2), and in so doing achieve . . . (*answer from 1*).

e.g. I will write and speak using my ability to inspire and motivate to accomplish peace and happiness and in so doing achieve happiness and fulfilment.

Now you have a mission statement that gives you a purpose and strengthens your sense of self. Feel free to repeat this exercise on a regular basis to fine-tune and hone. But it shouldn't change that dramatically. How you translate it into your life is up to you. You can infuse this ethos into everything you do and it will transform even the most routine day into something more potent.

Your New Vision for Life

What I want to ensure for you is that from this day onwards you have a sharper focus on that purpose and vision for your life. Your purpose is your Big Picture, a far-reaching vision for your life. It stems from the sense of being a part of something bigger than oneself and lends an overall sense of direction rather than leading to a particular goal or objective. Big Pictures have a tendency to sound rather grand and far-fetched so it is far better to live out that purpose, to demonstrate it, than to talk about it – at least in the early stages.

Passion and Calling

From the age of four to eighteen I was educated by the Sisters of Mercy in a convent in Ireland and it was a fascinating experience. Like nuns everywhere, my teachers were all following their 'calling'. They had been summoned by a Higher Power to do His work on earth and educate us girls as part of that vocation. They told us stories of their colleagues, the 'missionaries', working in the 'third world', feeding starving children, running schools and hospitals. I loved the idea of being singled out to dedicate my life to something important and worthwhile like this. Many's the time I sat alone in the school chapel, waiting to be called by the Lord Himself and given my orders, the purpose of my life revealed all in one succinct conversation. We were told there would be no mistaking or escaping the call. If He wanted us, we'd hear the call.

I never did have that particular conversation but the concept of living a passion-fuelled, purpose-driven life stayed with me. A flat life, safe in its day-to-dayness, has never appealed. I finished university with no clear sense of calling or passion for any particular route although there were obvious career moves I could have made, with great long-term prospects. Instead I left Ireland and worked as a waitress in a swanky London cocktail bar. And, yes, I see the irony now: waiting on tables while I waited for the call!

My call came in the shape of political campaigning. It wasn't an overnight dream or vision. I simply followed my passion for justice and fair play, joining the local Young Socialists group. I set up the South London Fair Fares campaign, defending Ken Livingstone's public transport policy, campaigned to save South London Women's Hospital, tried to stop cruise missiles coming to Greenham Common, raised money for the striking miners in 1984 and so on. I left the waitressing job to immerse myself totally in a counter-culture lifestyle, joining a 'not-for-profit' workers' co-operative running a wholefood shop, radical bookshop and vegetarian café. I became part of the collective that ran *Pavement*, London's longest-running community newspaper, and worked as an unpaid sleuth, writing front-page exclusives exposing the local Tory council's cover-up on asbestos on local housing estates and the like. Everything I did I felt passionate about, driven to do, and I very nearly made it to Nicaragua to help out during the revolution.

Eventually, my drive wore me out and I felt physically and emotionally exhausted. I knew I had to find a way of managing my passion without it consuming me so I took a step back from it all to re-evaluate what I should do next. Rebuilding my physical strength and restoring some *joie de vivre* in the search for other ways of living a meaningful life led me to explore and experiment with every alternative therapy around. For me, massage was heavenly, lifting my spirit at the same time as my stress. I had been intrigued by it ever since I first came across it – in the unlikely environs of a holding cell in Newbury police station! Locked up with twenty other Greenham Common protesters after a mass sit-down, one of the women carried out impromptu neck and shoulder treatments and I remember thinking what a smart skill that was.

To cut a longer story shorter, I did every massage and motivational course I could find. I discovered a brilliant practitioner called Fiona Shaw (not the actress!) who was to be my teacher and mentor for eighteen months. She had her own incredibly successful massage and self-esteem practice in central London, which was truly original and innovative. There was nothing else like her combination of massage and motivation available in London, or indeed anywhere, in the mid-1980s. This was the beginning of my coaching work, though the name had yet to be used in this way. I also set up the London College of Massage, selling it in 1994 to my then bookkeeper who was far more passionate about it than I had become.

I have often been asked how I had the foresight to know that massage and coaching would develop into the huge growth industries they have now become. The truth is, I didn't. I was only ever following my passion, what I was drawn to, felt enthusiastic about, thought was important and brought meaning and a sense of purpose to my life. So, what's your passion? This shouldn't be a daunting question – you just need to be honest with yourself and admit what you'd love to do if nothing stood in your way. Use the questions below to identify what really moves you.

What's Your Passion?

1. What would you do if you didn't have to earn a living? Imagine you've won the lottery, had a long holiday and are now keen to get back to work. What sort of things would you contemplate?

2. What activities are you happiest doing?

3. Identify three occasions when you've felt most alive, most powerfully and fully 'you'.

4. If you found yourself in prison for some time, what would you still continue to do?

5. What did you love to do when you were ten or younger?

Make the Dream a Reality

Being inspired by a dream is mentioned by many of the people I meet. This is dramatically true for Christina Noble, surely one of the most impressive people on earth, though that is the least of her concerns. Christina is the most down-to-earth person I have ever met. As a result of her dream, she established the Christina Noble Children's Foundation in Vietnam and Mongolia and has changed the lives of nearly 200,000 street children and their families. This is her story.

Christina Noble

It was in 1971 when I had the dream. I saw a road and a hole and a lot of children falling into the hole. They were Vietnamese. The word 'Vietnam' was written in the sky. One of them, a little girl, held out her hand to me. I could see the children running from the warred skies. I was in the dream, one of the kids if you like, in terms of expression and pain, and I could identify with their situation so clearly. Actually at the time I was running a fish-and-chip shop in Birmingham with my own three children to bring up and my youngest, Nicholas, was only a year old. I'd never been to Asia and knew absolutely nothing about the political situation. It's a very strange thing, but I never got into conversation with anyone about the dream or made a big deal about it at the time. My dream was something that stayed with me. That's all it was but I knew then that I would go to Vietnam to help children. It was as casual as that and was left at that, because there was something inside me that cannot be explained. And in many ways I didn't feel the need to explain it. Some people call it a vision. I don't know what it was but it left a very real imprint on my memory and I knew, when the time was right, I'd go.

It was while we were living in Surrey that it all started to happen. During that time I was studying drama, photography and painting as well as setting up my own catering company with very little money. That in itself became very successful out of nothing – just the determination to do it – but it was really just to keep us going. And so, in 1987, I began the process of trying to get out to Vietnam. In those days, it was incredibly difficult to get a visa. By 1989 I had met two brothers who were travelling out there on a regular basis. I told them that I was a magazine journalist and so I finally got in.

It was then that I witnessed at first hand kids sleeping on the streets at night. I remember seeing what appeared at first glance to be two tiny, skinny little girls playing with ants in the soil. What they were actually doing was eating ants. That was the start of it all for me – I connected that sight with my dream all those years before. I only needed to hold a little hand two or three times, like in my dream, and I made my spiritual connection. I don't have the words to explain it. This just had to be. I knew if I took that child's hand, I was signing a contract.

It took every possible resource and strength a human being has to make it happen. The easiest thing would have been to walk away. I thought about it many times. I'd go to bed, I couldn't sleep, I'd be sweating about what an impossible situation I was in. I mean, I had no education, no real contacts out there and didn't know the first thing about charities but I grew as a person over the years and really don't think I changed fundamentally.

I was born with a sensitivity to other human beings. As a child, growing up in the 1940s in the back streets of Dublin surrounded by terrible poverty, I was always so affected by the suffering I could see and felt automatically protective. What saved me, I think, was my talent for song and dance – I love theatre, jazz, blues. I used to love communicating on a stage to an audience through tap dancing. I always felt fortunate that I was given a gift/talent that would provide an escape from the squalor of the lives of impoverished people, the alcoholism and all that went with it for families in Ireland at that time. For a few moments in that concert hall, I felt special. For me, it was a real confidence builder of strength and character, which would eventually lead me to Ho Chi Minh City.

I told Shell and BP that the street people needed a medical centre and that these big multinationals should pay for it. Something told me to take their representatives downtown and show them the kids at first hand. I said: 'Don't tell me they're not worth fighting for – they could be your own flesh and blood.' I desperately wanted this medical/social centre and they gave me $10,000 to get it started. Now I needed to go to Hanoi to meet with the relevant authorities but I had nowhere to stay in that city so I slept rough in a dilapidated building with rats and bats, and what sounded like ghosts. I was absolutely terrified. I was meant to report my movements to the police in those days but I didn't. I took a big risk, but I was finally put in touch with the Ministry of Labour, Invalids and Social Affairs (MOLISA). I needed the permission of this organisation before I could go ahead. So what I did, I was completely honest, I told them all about my dream. I stated quite clearly that I literally only had my own heart to negotiate with, apart from the $10,000. That's all I had. They just had to give me the benefit of the doubt. I said they were welcome to my heart if it failed. That moved them. They respect and love me today.

It's very simple. There really is nothing complicated about what I felt. All children are entitled to housing, education and medical care. Each child deserves to know that there is somebody who cares about them. And so the medical centre got built and opened in 1991. We are currently in the process of redeveloping and modernising it. We now run a highly respected malnutrition centre, a nursery, a special care unit, and an outpatients department. We work closely with other hospitals that specialise in cancer, heart problems and paediatrics. Over the years we've built up incredible relationships. It's vital that all these services tie in with a child's schooling. We are the largest provider of flexible schooling in Vietnam for those kids who have no ID papers or who have to sell on the streets to support their families. We've set up sponsorship programmes. We make sure the water wells have electronic pumps. We have a chief international executive and officers in many different countries. The Christina Noble Children's Foundation (CNCF) is growing around the world and has won several awards.

We are now in the process of opening the first eco-house project in Ireland. Designed by the architect John Golding, this house is for disadvantaged children. They can use it to continue their education, learn how to budget, cook, clean, and join mainstream society. The aim is that in the future they will remember their early experiences and will have open hearts and minds. The best street educators are the ones who've lived on the streets themselves. It's about breaking that cycle of drugs, crime, brothels, child trafficking, etc. I believe in my heart and soul that this is going to turn things around in Northern Ireland. It's simple – about talking and listening.

I seized the moment. My success has only ever been measured in terms of the kids. I'm glad I did it. We have spread awareness of children's rights and haven't been afraid to speak out about sex abuse and the violation of human rights. I learnt that there are ways of doing this. You don't have to be a rebel; just speak the truth. I'm a mother and a child at the same time. These are the two qualifications I have. The rest is just hard work. I have always known that I can turn things around and make them work.

Christina's story of a housewife driven by a passion is incredible, but it is even more so when you look at where she's come from in life. Christina was born in a Dublin slum and was ten when her mother died and she and her five siblings were sent to different institutions. Beaten and abused, she ran away and lived on the streets. At 15 she was gang-raped and gave birth to a son, Thomas, who was taken from her and adopted. The fact that she managed to survive such an abusive and appalling childhood, Christina says, is a testimony to resilience – not only hers, but that of every human being – and her great empathy with street children is because she was once one herself. In seeing her life in this way, Christina is using every ounce of her experience to forge her success today, a success that has saved and changed the lives of many.

Your Passion and Destiny

You may already know what you are passionate about, or perhaps you've never really thought to ask the question, but either way, by now I hope you're feeling more connected to your passion. Clarifying and owning your passion is what's important at the moment – further on, we'll look at you taking action. And don't ever think it's too late to rediscover passion in your life and do something with it. I'll be introducing you to an amazing woman called Jibby Beane, later in the book, who did just that. In the meantime, consider the observation by Lester Burnham, played by Kevin Spacey in that wondrous film, *American Beauty*: 'Both my wife and daughter think I'm this gigantic loser, and they're right. I have lost something. I'm not exactly sure what it is, but I know I didn't always feel this sedated. But you know what? It's never too late to get it back.'

The notion of destiny is so seductive. But it can lead people into a state of apathy rather than control. Everyone wants to feel they're in touch with their destiny. How much of life is predestined and how much self-created? How much control do you really have? Do we come into the world a clean slate, for experience to stamp its mark on, or are we already imbued with a script? What is destiny after all? They say that 'luck is the meeting of preparation and opportunity'. I see destiny as the meeting of purpose, passion and preparation. There's talent involved too, but we'll come to that. I'm convinced that each of us has a purpose and that our personal talents and individual circumstances throughout life present us with the opportunities to fulfil that purpose. And it's not all about benefiting others and the world. It's about you, too; drawing out, and polishing, your private potential and personal refinement, as you grasp those opportunities, surmounting obstacles and disappointments.

Throughout history exceptional individuals have felt the hand of destiny guiding their success. On 3 July 2004 Maria Sharapova scored a breathtakingly audacious victory at the Wimbledon's ladies finals – and at 17 years old, became the third youngest women's champion in the tournament's history. She first picked up a racket at the age of four; left her mother and native Russia at six to train in Florida and at nine joined a bootcamp tennis academy, seeing her father once a week. Is destiny to be found here? You bet. Maria's success demonstrates the power of this combination of purpose, passion and preparedness. Add in talent and you're on destiny's path. Interestingly, this is what nine-times Wimbledon champion Martina Navratilova said: 'What a talent. She's been extremely committed to her cause, and she loves to play. That's the best part – she wants to be out there, she doesn't want to be anywhere else.'

What's your cause? It doesn't have to be international fame or sporting achievement, just something that you feel is inherently worthy. You must come to feel that you are manifesting your own destiny in your life. Otherwise, you could end up with a niggling feeling that something's missing, you're not quite where you should be, doing what you could be, thinking there must be more, perhaps asking yourself 'Is this all there is?'

The combination that leads to destiny is purpose, passion, preparedness and – talent.

What's Your Talent?

Every inspiring person you'll read about in these pages is talented. More importantly, they're using every drop of that talent. They're wringing full value out of the hand they've been dealt. Are you? Very few people that I come across, personally and professionally, even *see* their talents, let alone use them. Don't make the mistake of thinking that only some people are blessed with talent. That's nonsense and serves as a useful excuse for not making full use of yourself. We all get our fair share of talent: what we make of it is down to us. That's the beauty and the challenge of free will. Forget about fate.

Remember the happiness expert, Dr Seligman, and his life's research, pointing to the importance of using your 'signature strengths'? I prefer the word 'talents', but we're both talking about that unique combination of abilities and aptitudes that make you, 'you'. I'm looking for your intrinsic, essential talents, as opposed to the more obvious skills and formal qualifications that you may have earned along the way. I find it more interesting and relevant to a successful life to look at what you're fundamentally 'designed' to be great at. I want you to be your own talent scout, and here's a clue – look to your passion first. Would Maria Sharapova's success be possible without passion driving her? Passion and talent are invariably linked.

Your talents, your signature strengths, may not be as specific as tennis. You may have outstanding attributes like the ability to motivate or manage people. You may be one of those 'born leaders', with an inherent ability to connect with people and inspire them to achieve great things. Kally Ellis's most important talent may not be actual floral designs – that's her business partner Ercole's strength – but she is talented in other areas.

Talent and Training

Whatever your personal strengths are, they'll have been a part of your make-up for ever. You may want to hone and perfect them but, essentially, you've just got that talent. Clearly, your choice of profession may require you to take formal training and demonstrate your 'qualification' for the job. And obviously I would feel more comfortable about a highly trained heart surgeon operating on me than an untrained enthusiast. But I'd still look for the passionate, driven one, as that's where you'll find the talent as well.

Don't get obsessive about 'qualifications'. There is so much that you can do that relies on your intrinsic talent and application, whereas years spent studying not only wastes time but could teach you 'rules' that actually constrict your flair and creativity. In the following pages you'll read about Maria Grachvogel, the fashion designer who eschewed years of formal training, preferring to learn as she practised and worked. Had she trained, one of the 'rules' she would have learnt would have been to delegate pattern cutting to a pattern-cutting expert. As it is, it never occurred to her not to do her own pattern cutting and this is still a hugely important part of the design process for her.

I hate to see talent and potential go to waste, especially when someone is truly passionate about something. I came across a blatant example of this in a recent seminar, where I was coaching people to move their life on to their next level. Jennifer was an attractive, stylish thirtysomething, newly divorced with girls of nine and eleven. She really needed to earn more money and find an interesting career. Helping out at her daughters' school as a classroom assistant paid very little and, though worthwhile, wasn't the career she yearned for. When I quizzed her about her interests and passions, she came alive, talking about her home and how gorgeous she had made it. She had increased the value significantly through the improvements she'd made, and she adored nothing more than making rooms and houses exquisite places to be in.

It transpired that she had been playing around with home improvement for as long as she could remember, rearranging the furniture in the family home as soon as her parents went out for the evening. I really wanted to wake her up to her talent and the life that was just waiting for her to set up. A failure to appreciate her own gifts and the feeling that she needed to be 'qualified' before she could offer her services commercially kept her stuck and frustrated, with her talent languishing and wasted. I sketched out for her the potential life available to her, describing how she could offer a house doctor/home makeover service for the cash-rich, time-challenged commuters in her neighbourhood, turning their 'houses into homes' or helping them sell their properties quickly, for the maximum price.

I pointed out the incredible success of the TV programme, *House Doctor*, as evidence of our appetite and awareness for home makeovers and improvements: reminding her that the fabulous house doctor, Ann Maurice, had not taken a degree in house doctoring (there isn't one!) and had in fact been a real estate agent in San Francisco prior to her Channel 5 success. I'm not sure that Jennifer was ready to shake herself to be a bit bolder in her outlook. One thing's for sure – only she could declare herself 'qualified' and open for business. Until then she would keep her talent hidden, for her own private use, rather than risk going public and putting it to work for her.

As the legendary choreographer George Balanchine would say to a lazy or leisurely dancer, 'What are you saving yourself for?' It's time to identify your talents. Use the questions below to pinpoint the things you're intrinsically good at.

Spot Your Talents

1. When you were a child, how did you imagine yourself as an adult?
What did you see yourself doing?

2. What did you enjoy most at school? What were you best at?
How much of these activities do you do now?

3. What do you see as your signature strengths?

4. In which situations do you feel most 'yourself?'

What, precisely, are you doing when you feel most yourself?

5. What do people admire or envy you for?

6. What comes easily to you?

7. What resources do you have to offer?

8. Which three words best describe how you see yourself?

9. What is unique about you?

10. Putting modesty aside, make a list of what you consider to be your genuine talents, regardless of any improvements you think they could benefit from.

A Lifelong Passion

Having a vision for your life doesn't have to come in a dream. Some people have a passion that is evident to them from the outset. This is true of Maria Grachvogel, who at 34 has become one of London's most talked-about and exciting designers. Totally self-taught, and self-funded, her designs are adored by British showbiz personalities. Victoria Beckham has even modelled on the catwalk for her and Emma Thompson recently reinvented herself as a Hollywood siren in Maria Grachvogel designs. In 2001 Maria opened her own flagship store on London's Sloane Street.

Maria Grachvogel

I have always been very, very focused. This was always my heart-and-soul dream. At eight years old, I began sketching and making catalogues, when I was 12 I taught myself to sew and by 14, I was cutting patterns and making my first proper collection for friends. One thing that really struck me was that everything looked the same. I didn't want to be put in a box. I wanted to be free to be creative and the only place to achieve that was Central St Martin's School of Art – which would have taken a couple of years to qualify for.

I was impatient. So I attended an evening business course specifically aimed at the fashion industry and worked in D. R. Harris in St James's, the oldest chemist and perfumery in London, during the day. I remember dressing the window with these beautiful ivory hairbrushes which had been hidden in the stockroom for years because they weren't selling. Within a day of my display, they were selling for £600 each. Whatever I put in their shop window sold immediately. I totally loved it.

To work for someone else was never in my sphere of thought. But if my ambition was to succeed, I needed to make more money. So I took a job in the City as a filing clerk. I progressed rapidly and within a month or so was entered for the Stock Exchange exams. Although this wasn't part of my plan, I became the youngest person to pass! This was somewhat ironic because actually all I ever wanted to be was a fashion designer. I stayed as an investment assistant for about six months as I knew it was a good thing to be learning so much about finance and I did find it really interesting.

When I left, I set up a joint venture with my best friend from school. It was a tiny, made-to-order-from-sketches, company; all private client work, word of mouth and local advertising, operating from my parents' house. I financed it entirely from the monies I'd saved religiously since I was eight. It lasted a couple of years and I learnt a very valuable lesson. Its downfall was due to my partner's total lack of commitment and honesty. This constituted my first major learning curve in business because I had wrongly believed that I needed a partner to share the responsibility with. So, after another short spell in the City at Schroders, I started again.

In January 1991 I set up Maria Grachvogel, designing a small first collection of nine pieces. Through a contact I'd made from my days in the City, I was introduced to Lucienne Phillips, who owned a shop in Knightsbridge selling the latest, hip young designers of the time. Being a fierce Frenchwoman, she gave me five minutes to prove myself. I started off modelling one of my dresses (it is soooo uncool for a designer to model her own clothing, I later discovered!).

And she wrote my first order – for everything! I was amazed and uplifted and she remained a special client of mine until she retired. Over the next four years, I built up a series of small wholesale orders and private clients. In 1994 I received my small first order from Liberty and the next year I presented my first catwalk show at London Fashion Week. All this was still totally self-funded.

It is really important to have total creative freedom. I design and make glamorous, wearable clothing. I didn't want to go the shock-value route. Business has built gradually over the years. If you get a backer too early, then they call the shots. I feel, for example, that pattern cutting is an important part of the creative process and so have always done that myself. This comes from being self-taught. Although a chance comment from Clements Ribiero taught me that no one actually cuts their own patterns!

You never stop learning when you have your own business. In 2001 I opened my shop on Sloane Street, but I have to say, it's been the biggest challenge of all. I'm such a sensitive person and have invested an awful lot of trust in people. I now realise that some people will take advantage of that. In certain situations, I find people very draining. The downfall is that I tend to think everyone works like me. I expect so much of people and I'm aware it's hard to live up to that. I found it difficult to be designer/creator/cutter as well as staff manager, which I don't really enjoy due to my lack of patience The extraordinary thing is that the minute I started letting things bog me down, the synchronicity stopped. I've really struggled to find the right person to help me run the business so I can let go a bit.

At heart, I am passionate about what I do, and I hope everyone – from the customers to the girls who work in the shop – can feel that. I can't help but get excited. It's not just about clothes; I love making women feel fabulous. I do dress a lot of celebrities but I've never courted them. I even remember asking Victoria Beckham who the Spice Girls were! They come to me for the same reason everyone does – my clothes make them feel beautiful.

On the day that I met Maria she had been in the headlines for dressing Emma Thompson and the papers and style pundits were desperate to know how the actress had been transformed. Some suggested punishing two-hour daily workouts, others expensive facials, but the truth lay in the dress hanging on a rail by my side in Maria's gorgeous shop. Looking around I spotted others that were familiar from previous front pages and in that instant I grasped that this was Maria's dream come true, a vision of her life that she'd held from the age of eight. That vision was not to be famous for her clientele, but to be a truly successful designer, recognised and acknowledged for her talent. I loved the fact that she was entirely self-taught and had been working steadfastly towards this, and saving money to fund it too, throughout her life.

Notice how her passion has fuelled her incredible determination and achievement. To have your own shop in Sloane

Street, debt and loan free, entirely paid for from your own hard work, passion and talent is an incredible achievement.

Passion really does galvanise us to become bigger, bolder people. It feeds and sustains us through the most difficult times. It makes sense of sacrifice and hardship, keeping self-pity in check until success arrives. My next successful person is a world away from Maria in that his passion is for human rights but, like Maria, this has been his path and purpose since he was a child. I first became aware of Peter Tatchell in the early 1980s, when we were both political activists and Labour Party members. We both lived in south London, he in Bermondsey, I in Tooting, but we never met. When it looked for a moment as if he might actually make it to Parliament as an MP, there was a feeling of sheer revolution in the air. A few years later, I became worn out by all the struggle and stepped back from frontline campaigning. Peter, however, has not. Over the years I have marvelled at how he could sustain his passion and energy. He has influenced so many people's lives and been responsible for numerous changes in the law. Most recently he successfully campaigned to persuade leading reggae labels not to promote homophobic songs. Always a controversial figure, even among the gay community, he remains undiminished and irrepressible to this day.

Peter Tatchell

I was born in 1952 in Melbourne, at a time when homosexuality was totally illegal. There's nobody in my family like me. They live in Australia and are working-class suburbanites with low expectations and no real aspirations. My parents are very religious and instilled in me a very strong sense of right and wrong. But they were mostly preoccupied with avoiding sins like swearing, dancing and having sex before marriage, whereas I interpreted Christ's gospel as liberation theology. I translated those values into a social conscience and social activism.

Gay men could be jailed and forced by courts to undergo psychiatric treatment. I moved to London in 1971 and joined the newly formed Gay Liberation Front. Homophobia was also rife in the UK. Inspired by Mahatma Gandhi, Sylvia Pankhurst, Martin Luther King and Malcolm X, I began adopting direct-action methods of protest. Shock tactics are often necessary to expose injustice and kick-start reform. Doing a direct-action protest is incredibly nerve-racking. I have done thousands over the last four decades, but my stomach still churns every time.

There have been non-stop hate mail, death threats, obscene telephone calls and attacks on my home – including bricks and bullets through the front door and windows; plus more than five hundred assaults in the street over the last twenty years. Most of my teeth are chipped and cracked from the bashings. They began in 1981 when I was selected as the Labour candidate for Bermondsey in south London. Much of the violence has been by organised neo-Nazi gangs like the National Front, the British National Party and Combat 18, but recently some has come from Islamic fundamentalists.

My one-bedroom flat in Elephant and Castle is protected like a fortress: all the door and window frames are reinforced and there are fire extinguishers in every room. I would love to live somewhere safer, but doing paid work would take me away from my human rights campaigning and divert my energy from effecting political and cultural change.

Anybody experiencing great difficulties has self-doubts and occasional thoughts of giving it all up and walking away. What keeps me going is a belief that what I'm doing is necessary and seeing the positive end results. I know from messages people send me that I've helped change their lives for the better. Securing changes in legislation and government policy is also a great motivator. Each success inspires me to bigger and bolder campaigns.

In 1989, the number of gay men convicted of the consensual offence of gross indecency rocketed to a level almost as great as in 1954 at the height of the anti-gay witch-hunts, when homosexuality was still totally illegal. Polite negotiations with the police failed. Working with the gay rights' group OutRage!, I organised a series of direct-action protests to challenge the police victimisation of the gay community. We invaded police stations, busted undercover entrapment operations and disrupted press conferences being held by the Metropolitan Police Commissioner.

Within three months, the police were sitting down with us and beginning serious negotiations. Within a year, they had agreed to most of our demands for a non-homophobic policing policy. Less than three years later, the number of gay men convicted of this victimless offence had fallen by two-thirds: the biggest and fastest fall ever. We helped save thousands of gay men from being arrested, dragged through the courts, getting a criminal conviction and having their career prospects blighted. When I think about that positive achievement, it gives me the inspiration to keep going in the face of any adversity.

With a bit of determination and imagination it can be quite easy to bring about change. Each success has encouraged me to aim for further success. Sometimes you don't succeed. That's part of life. But I've never been deterred by a knock back. I always take note of why things didn't work and try to learn from my mistakes.

There have been moments when I've felt very downhearted. For about ten years, much of the media declared open season. I was vilified and misrepresented relentlessly. Even I didn't like the Peter Tatchell I was reading about!

The coverage of the 'outing' campaign in the early 1990s was probably the worst example of media misrepresentation in Britain. They claimed we were outing innocent, harmless bishops because they were gay; we weren't. It was because they were attacking the gay community in public while having gay affairs in private. We were naming and shaming them because they were two-faced hypocrites – and homophobes. But that truth was never reported. I felt totally and utterly powerless. Most papers wouldn't even publish a letter from me refuting their lies. Even among the gay community, there was considerable hostility towards the campaign. The thought of giving up entered my head for a moment or two, but I soon dismissed it. It would be cowardly and a betrayal of my own principles to run away. I just kept saying to myself, 'I know what I stand for, I know what I've done; if others choose to ignore and distort that, it's their problem.' My reasoning was: if I remain true to my beliefs and maintain my campaigns, eventually even my harshest critics will either give up or accord me a degree of grudging respect.

I make about £8,000 a year from writing and broadcasting, but my human rights work is unpaid. What I lack in material and financial rewards, I am more than compensated for psychologically and emotionally by the positive feedback that I get from people I've helped – and from the successes of the campaigns I've organised.

I was keen to meet Peter in person for the first time. Our lives had taken very different courses in the twenty years that had passed since my activist days. As I waited for him to arrive in the hotel bar, I imagined him to be just a tad world-weary, battle-scarred and bitter. *Au contraire*. He strode in and heads turned. The man had real presence and charisma. He was fresh, youthful and vital, looking at least ten years younger than his 53 years. I was intrigued. My first question was: How on earth did he manage to maintain such a vibrant spirit and upbeat air, not to mention looking so good? He replied that he felt incredibly content with his life and all that he had achieved so far. It wasn't just his passion that fuelled him; he genuinely felt thrilled at the difference he'd made, and continued to make, to people's lives. Living on £8,000 a year, he had a greater feeling of success than many people earning ten times that amount. As a coach, I've worked with numerous people who earn serious amounts of money but don't feel successful. They may feel trapped in a job they loathe, or regret that they've missed out on so much of their children's lives, or else the sheer stress of their career has undermined their health. They talk of not being true to themselves, not following their heart or making the most of life. Such dissatisfaction is a terrible burden to live with.

After we'd finished talking and I'd turned off my tape recorder, I was still left with one question: What had sparked off this passion in the first place? It clearly wasn't Peter's parents, teachers or peers. I felt *something* must have happened to put him on this path. I persisted and here's the answer.

In 1965, when Peter was 13, there was an attempted breakout from Melbourne's prison, Pentridge. A warden was shot dead while pursuing one of the escaped prisoners, Ronald Ryan. Ryan was charged with the murder. Reading press reports, Peter noted that the bullet had entered through the top of the warden's back. He immediately figured that the entry and exit points of the bullet meant the gun must have been fired from above and behind, making it impossible for Ryan to have fired the fatal shot. The warden was almost certainly shot accidentally by one of the other wardens, probably on a watchtower. Peter wrote to the paper pointing this out, but the letter was ignored. Frustrated, he began his own one-man, do-it-yourself campaign, daubing 'Save Ryan' and 'Ryan is Innocent' slogans on the railway bridges, bus shelters and walls of suburban Melbourne.

Ronald Ryan was hanged in 1967 for a crime he probably never committed. Three decades later, long after Peter had left Melbourne, an inquiry concluded that the trajectory of the bullet meant it was most likely to have been fired by another warden. The then premier of Victoria, Henry Bolte, had used the case to bolster his tough-on-crime stance, ignoring the evidence that would have saved Ryan. Peter witnessed all this at the age of 13 and was so incensed by the obvious injustice meted out to one prisoner that his desire for justice and fair play was activated from that moment onwards.

Perhaps there have been moments in your own life that have activated a passion or provoked a sense of outrage that has spurred you into action, too? If not, look around you to see what you feel moved to improve. You don't have to give your life over to your chosen cause like Peter, but could incorporate it into your current activities. A hidden benefit is the close communication you'll find with others who share your passion. Don't sit and wait for a passionate life to happen to you. Go looking for it. Join in.

Five Steps for Greater Passion

1. Find a passion. Go and do something you feel passionate about. Identify a cause you feel strongly about that will get more passion flowing through your veins. Ensure that it aligns with your purpose and incorporates your talents.

2. Reduce what drains you. List everything and everyone in your life that lowers your energy. Figure out a way to eliminate these influences or reduce their role in your life.

3. Do something different. Energise your life by organising a group of friends or acquaintances to get together. It could be a salsa class or you could perhaps start a club. Try a book club, wine club or a supper club, where everyone cooks a different course and you all eat together.

4. Study kindred spirits. Make a list of the lives of people who have known their purpose and followed their passion. Who do you admire the most? Read biographies of these people and explore how they maintained their purpose and passion when obstacles surfaced.

5. Appreciate yourself – passionately! No one has greater power to increase or diminish your *joie de vivre* than you. Look over your list of talents regularly and feel lucky to have been blessed with your particular combination. There's no one quite like you on this planet and there never will be. Now that is something to get excited about. Make sure you do.

2: *Practise* **SELF-BELIEF**

You have to have self-belief to get anywhere in life. Where you end up is where your self-belief takes you to. You are the product of all that you believe to be possible for you. It really is that simple and it really is all in the mind.

I used to believe there was a formula for self-belief. I still do, but I've changed my mind about what that is. I used to think that a combination of the right parents and the right early influences would set you up for life; that you had a strong core of self-belief embedded within you from the outset and were advantaged from the start. It's five years since my book, *Be Your Own Life Coach*, was published and in that time I have been prompted to reconsider this perspective. Having worked with thousands of people in talks, presentations and personal sessions, I no longer think it's that straightforward because I've seen too much evidence which challenges my old belief.

In a nutshell, I've met too many individuals who have had these right influences yet lacked the strong core of self-belief you'd expect to find. And I've encountered so many others who have, on paper, had a disastrous start in life but who are invincible. So, the formula works for some but not for all. I can't guarantee it. The inescapable conclusion I've come to is this: self-belief is self-created. The meaning of life and its direction is more down to you than even *I* thought.

My experience as a life coach convinces me that your life is in your hands, or rather in your mind. It's determined by free will and this was what was missing from my earlier perspective. Free will gives us the capacity to choose how we create our lives, exercise our ability to be self-determined. Free will is the will not to conform to the past and it's the measure of a person's capacity to act as an individual.

The world is full of people whose experiences illustrate the primary importance and power of free will. Consider Bill Clinton and George Bush, the former and current presidents of the United States, who grew up in extremely different environments. Bush came from an oil-rich, Texan family, the son of a former US president, so no surprises when he ended up in the White House himself. Bill Clinton's father died when his mother was six months pregnant with him, and he spent his early years in terrible poverty, with an abusive, alcoholic stepfather, in Little Rock, Arkansas. Yet he rose to become leader of the most powerful nation on earth. Forget his politics. The man is a model of self-determination, allowing neither his past nor his circumstances to dictate his future or his character. A measure of his strength and poise lies in the fact that, as he turned 14, he stood up to his stepfather, telling him that he must never lift a hand to beat his mother again. Nor did he.

But the world is full of individuals with similar starts in life who have been crushed and defeated by their environment and become resigned to a dismal fate. The difference lies in the extent to which people are prepared to resist their circumstances and exert their will to make change.

On the other hand, I have coached numerous individuals from the 'right' side of the tracks who have had all those favourable influences yet had the most abysmally low stock of self-belief. I remember Elizabeth, a smart young woman, complaining that her loving, secure upbringing and well-connected, urbane parents had made her life 'too comfortable': the fact that she would never starve if she didn't earn her own living, she felt, deprived her of any real incentive. She figured that if she lived in a run-down council flat, relying on state benefits, perhaps she would have serious motivation to write that novel, get that deal, really make things happen. She felt she just wasn't hungry enough. She was ambitious, had dreams, but used her circumstances to explain why she was not likely to succeed. I called a halt to the coaching on our third session, suggesting that she return when she was ready to give up her 'story' and get on with creating her life. As I write, nothing has changed in her situation.

This perspective is no better and no worse than that of the resigned individual from the 'wrong' side of the tracks. Both are self-defeated, both victims of their circumstances, of their own making. Both deny the option of free will, shying away from the freedom and opportunity of self-determination.

Free Will vs. Fate

There are only two attitudes available to any of us when we are squaring up to life. One is embracing free will. The other is a belief in fate. More accurately, your interpretation of fate. My position is that free will operates at every level of our lives, that we even choose where and when to incarnate, in order to develop our selves, our souls more fully. I believe this decision is taken in co-operation with God, the gods, a Higher Power, call it what you will, so that the life we opt for is the one we will ultimately learn and benefit most from. So, fate and destiny exist with our full support and agreement. Nothing is forced upon us, against our will. We are not at the mercy of any outside force, however celestial. The extent to which we feel we're living out our destiny is the extent to which we've picked up the gauntlet of free will and run with it to meet life head on, valuing every experience, great or gruesome. Then it starts to feel 'right'. We're living the life we 'should' be living, on the right track, the right path.

Astrology is wonderful for gaining greater insight into your inner workings, impulses and desires. And, if you accept my premise of a freely chosen incarnation, then the time and place of your birth is not random or accidental. I learnt this for myself when I had my astrological chart interpreted by a well-known astrologer many years ago. She said my chart could only belong to someone born into a place such as Northern Ireland or the Lebanon, somewhere plagued by tremendous conflict and violence, a war zone, which was what Northern Ireland was to become as I turned ten. My older brother Brian was a student at Queen's University in Belfast as the civil rights movement erupted and I joined him on all the early marches and demonstrations, finding the charged atmosphere compulsive. 'The Troubles', as they became known, would be a feature of my life from then on. We were driven out of our home on a predominantly Protestant housing estate because we were Catholics but we were lucky not to have been 'burnt out' as some of our neighbours had been.

Tolerance has never been my strongest point, nor is it to this day. But what more ideal place and time could I have been born into in order to witness the repercussions of rampant intolerance? Growing up in a place where people killed and tortured each other because they refused to tolerate and accommodate to their differences gave me a unique vantage point from which to study intolerance. I believe I was born in Northern Ireland and lived through the Troubles for a reason.

The mistake that some people make is in waiting for destiny to deliver the goods, or in feeling that fate or an unlucky planetary alignment has condemned them to conditions or a life they would rather not have. This is a convenient but distorted reading of these forces. The phenomenally successful television star Oprah Winfrey has the right idea when she says, 'I don't think of myself as a poor deprived ghetto girl who made good. I think of myself as somebody who, from an early age, knew I was responsible for myself and I had to make good.'

Another magnificent woman who thinks along these lines is Barbara Corcoran. Barbara grew up in New Jersey, sharing one floor in a three-family house with her parents and nine brothers and sisters. She had few luxuries, but she was blessed with a mother who taught her to see that she had as much going for her as anyone, rather than viewing herself as a poor girl stuck in Edgewater. After failing at twenty-two other jobs, Barbara, at 56, is known as the 'Queen of New York Real Estate'. Celebrity clients have included Madonna, Harrison Ford and Robin Williams and with sales volume at over $9 billion in 2004, the Corcoran Group is New York's leading real estate company. Exactly how did the waitress from New Jersey become one of the most powerful figures in New York City real estate?

Barbara Corcoran

My mom had a genius for putting her finger on the special gift she saw in each of her ten kids and making every one of us believe that that gift was uniquely ours. The trick was then to apply that gift to your advantage. That's what I can put my success down to, knowing what I had going for me and using it.

Let me tell you about the first time I really applied that lesson. I was 21, living at home in Edgewater, New Jersey, and working as a waitress at the Fort Lee Diner. On my first day at the diner, my heart sank when I saw Gloria, the other waitress. She had assets that I'd never have, at least without surgical support. That night I went home to fret to my mother: 'And when we weren't busy, Mom, my counter was plain empty. Even when Gloria's station was completely filled, men were still asking to sit with Gloria and not me.' Mom replied, 'Barbara Ann, you've got a great personality. You're going to have to learn to use what you've got. Since you don't have big breasts, why don't you tie some ribbons on your pigtails and just be as sweet as you are.'

And that's how it was. I wore ribbons on my pigtails and

offered a cheerful alternative to the big-breasted, blonde-bombshell Fort Lee sensation. Customers walked in and asked to sit with 'pigtails' and my sweet-talking kept them coming back. Two years down the line, one of those customers, Ramone Simone, was to be my ticket out of Fort Lee and across the river into New York. Ray said a smart girl like me should be living in the Big City and offered to pay for me to spend a week at the Barbizon Hotel for Women.

This was my chance to run my own show and find a place of my own and I grabbed it. Within a week I had found an apartment and had landed a receptionist's job with Giffuni Brothers, two wealthy landlords who owned a dozen apartment buildings in Manhattan and Brooklyn. This gave me my introduction to Manhattan real estate and after a few months I convinced Ray to loan me $1,000 to start a real estate company. He agreed on condition that he had the controlling interest in the business. My old boss, Joseph Giffuni, said he would pay me a whole month's rent as commission if I could find a tenant for one of his apartments.

Mr Giffuni's apartment was no different from the 1,246 other one-bedroom apartments advertised in that Sunday's New York Times. *How, I asked myself, could I put ribbons on a typical one-bedroom in four lines or less and make it stand out from the other 1,246 apartments? I persuaded Mr Giffuni to put up a wall separating the living room from the dining alcove. That way he'd have something different to market and be able to rent it for twenty dollars more each month. He had the wall installed that week and a few days later my ad went into the paper, offering a one-bedroom* with a den. *It wasn't a big ad, but it offered something extra. Why would anyone settle for a one-bedroom, when for the same price you could get a one-bedroom* with a den*? That Sunday, the calls began. And on Monday I rented my first apartment.*

I saw that good salesmanship was nothing more than maximising the positive and minimizing the negative. Although

> *your competition might offer something you can't match, that isn't important. What matters is that you identify and play up what you've got. I didn't have a big chest, but I did have a nice personality, a great smile, and the gift of the gab.*

I first came across Barbara on a trip to New York. There was no missing her, as she was plastered on billboards from Madison Avenue to Times Square. It was April 2003 and her book, *Use What You've Got and Other Business Lessons I Learned from My Mom*, was on the *New York Times* best-seller list (now available in paperback as *If You Don't Have Big Breasts, Put Ribbons on Your Pigtails*) and Barnes & Noble had copies stacked high on tables as you walked in. That evening as I hit the treadmill in the hotel gym, there was the author, up on the television screen doing a slot on the *60 Minutes* show! I bought her book the next day, loved it, and called 'her people' to arrange a meeting. She seemed such a formidable figure, the 'Doyenne of Manhattan Real Estate', as one newspaper called her, that I figured she'd be terrifying to interview. What a pleasant surprise awaited me. From the moment we spoke I saw exactly what her mother had been getting at: she had the sweetest personality you could ever have and was incredibly, well, *nice*. I liked her immensely and could see how she would have easily won over Donald Trump or any other New York mogul just by using what she had, her 'gift of the gab' as her Irish American mother put it.

Use What You've Got

Barbara believed herself to be equal to anyone. It never occurred to her that she was defined or diminished by her background. If she personifies the American Dream, it's because of this deep-rooted self-belief. Her success was built on using her assets to the full in her approach to every stage and every challenge of her life. She used her way with people to make her way in life, beginning with the initial change of attitude in her waitressing job to ensure that she established a friendly rapport with all her customers. And, four years later, it would be one of those customers who would provide the stepping-stone for her move out of Edgewater into a bigger world. Her gutsiness ensured that she had secured a job and a room for herself in mid-town Manhattan before her borrowed money ran out. Observe how simple yet brilliant her strategy was in continually emphasising the unique selling point of everything she needed to sell, from the very first apartment that was to launch her real estate career. As soon as she could afford to advertise, she was also unique in including her friendly face in the box ads she placed, which made her stand out on a page crammed with small ads, personalising the business to a prospective customer. Nowadays she does exactly the same, except that her short blonde hair and all-American smile beams at you from 30-foot-high posters right across the city and the company which she started with a $1,000 loan was sold in 2001 for a reputed $70 million.

Resist the temptation to see only what you feel is missing. Focus instead on seeing and using what you've got. Don't waste time or energy wishing you were someone else, had someone else's lot, otherwise your own lot will go to waste. You've got enough going for you as you are. See it, and see it that way.

Pre-determined vs. Self-determined

You don't have to share my exact beliefs on the meaning and purpose of life, but I urge you to embrace self-determination and create your life with enthusiasm and confidence. The reward of self-determination is that you need never be a victim of circumstances, never be at the mercy of your past or conditioning to determine who you are and the course of your life.

Journalist John McCarthy was kidnapped in 1986 and held for five years in Lebanon. Until he was kidnapped he had lived a comfortable, happy life in London, 'so to be plunged into a desperate situation, where you find yourself not in control of your own destiny, and there is not even a handle on the inside of the door of the room you are kept in, woke me up to what other people have to go through on a daily basis. Beirut sensitised me to other people's suffering.' John forged a profound meaning from the experience of being locked in that room and others like it, which he now uses in his work as patron of the Medical Foundation for the Care of Victims of Torture.

Even if your situation is not as extreme as this, you will undoubtedly encounter difficulties in your life, some of them very challenging. But you are never a victim of circumstances because you are always free to choose your response. What matters most is not your experience, but how you respond to what you experience in life.

What Do You Believe About Yourself?

This is a brainstorming exercise. Complete the statements rapidly, without censoring or analysing your answers.

1. One of my biggest regrets about my childhood is . . .

2. What I would go back and change if I could is . . .

3. What I missed out on when I was growing up was . . .

4. If I'd had a better start in life, then I'd be . . .

5. With more support and encouragement I could have been . . .

Process Your Beliefs

Do the answers in this exercise surprise you? In theory, the ideal outcome is to draw blanks with each statement, which would indicate that you do not feel in the slightest determined, or restricted by, the circumstances of your life. If you were able to complete the statements, then you have work to do in shifting your position from determined to self-determined. You have yet to sign up for full membership of the free-will club. Mind you, if this is the case, you are not alone as there are very few of us who don't have some 'if onlys' in our vocabulary. Just the other day I was horrified to find myself thinking along those lines. I caught myself imagining where I might be now if I'd had a different start in life, if I'd been born to affluent, well-connected parents in London. I immediately reminded myself that my own start was absolutely perfect in giving me the opportunity to realise my own potential. Eternal vigilance is the only answer!

Your reward for subscribing to self-determination and free will is exceptional, lifelong self-belief. Here's why. The extent to which you believe others, or something else, to be responsible for the circumstances of your life is the extent to which you deny yourself access to your own resources, capabilities and ingenuity. When there is someone or something to blame, whether you were too rich or too poor, too much loved or not loved enough, you're excusing yourself and resisting the challenge of making your life work. Crucially, you could be missing out on making use of the advantages you actually have available to you as a result of those experiences. One of the smartest things you can do is to see yourself as 'advantaged'. And this has nothing to do with going to Eton or Harrow, Columbia or Yale, holidaying in the Hamptons or skiing in St Moritz.

Enjoy Your Advantages

What are your advantages in life? Here's how to find them. Look back to the exercise you've just completed, to the 'if only' stuff. Remember I said that, in theory, it would be ideal to draw blanks? Well, in practice, your advantage is concealed in that disappointment, regret or resentment. If you have a clean sheet for this exercise, you're probably already seeing and making full use of your advantages. Congratulations for being so exceptional and take another look for yet more advantages. For everyone else, the challenge is simple: to spot the hidden advantage in everything that's ever happened to you, especially when it's well hidden, wrapped up in regret or resentment.

Take an inventory of how you see things. Can you change the way you see them? Can you see potential benefit where you've previously seen loss? Can you change the way you feel about something simply by changing the way you see it? Can you use a shift in perspective to make something work in your favour rather than against you? The answer is: absolutely. Self-determined people do this automatically. But it's a habit any one of us can acquire at any time we choose.

The name of this habit is gratitude. You'll see what I mean when you carry out the exercise to identify your advantages, and the source of them. No other habit gives you the same opportunity, freedom and peace of mind. There's only one rule and it's to spot the opportunity in your experiences and put them to good use for your own personal refinement and happiness. If you're new to this way of thinking, just keep an open mind, keep processing your beliefs and encouraging yourself to think along these lines. In looking for lessons, remember you're only interested in 'useful' ones. It's not a useful lesson if you use it to shut down, contract or diminish your stature. For example, declaring that you've learnt a valuable lesson never to lend anyone money again, when a friend doesn't repay you, makes you a smaller, not a smarter person.

I respect that you may have had some terrible things happen to you but I want to encourage you to put all the wisdom and insight available to you to good use for your benefit. Recovering from the death of a loved one, for example, especially a child, is a colossal event, which can really stop people in their tracks for a long time, sometimes for ever. Taking something from that experience can feel impossible, but our recovery may depend on us extracting some meaning out of that loss.

Use Your Advantage

Complete this exercise to rethink the meaning and significance of past events. Take one incident or issue that you wish you could change. Now answer these short questions:

1. Something useful I learnt about myself from that experience was . . .

2. A smart way I can make that insight work for me in my life is . . .

3. The way in which that experience makes me unique is . . .

4. The opportunity that experience gave me was . . .

5. Making full use of that advantage would mean . . .

Self-belief and Gratitude

I met someone recently at a dinner party whose gratitude for some horrendously traumatic experiences amazed me. At 42,

Gary is a successful London make-up artist working with the top glossy magazines, doing all the big fashion shows in New York, Paris and Milan. He oozes bonhomie and really is the person you'd want to sit next to at a dinner party. He has a great lifestyle, terrific friends and is one of the most attractive people I've ever met.

We got talking and he told me about his childhood in the English countryside. He explained how he felt 'different' from other children as he was growing up. Without understanding it, he had an inkling that he was gay. He had no notion of gayness to relate to, had never met a gay person or knew of their existence. He felt a freak and yearned to be 'normal'. His devoted parents determined to do everything they could to find a 'cure'. They took him to doctors and psychiatrists. This led to counselling and eventually a course of electric convulsive therapy (ECT) where he was held down and strapped to a chair while the shocks were administered. Pictures of naked men and women were shown to him at various points in the hope of triggering his brain to function 'normally'.

As I looked increasingly horrified, he rushed to reassure me that everything was done to help him get 'better', which he dearly wanted, with his consent. His parents and the medical experts were trying to rewire his brain for his benefit. Sure, a few of the 'experts' involved had been vicious in their treatment of him, but the majority were just eager to help him.

He went on to explain the advantages these events had brought him. He grew up feeling uncomfortable about being gay and as a result was not 'out there' in his twenties, having sexual relationships. This would have been in the 1980s, at the height of the Aids epidemic. He felt lucky that he had missed that era of promiscuity, and now he was dating in his forties at a time of much greater awareness of safe sex. Huge numbers of gay men died during those years and he could have been one of them. Another advantage he saw was that while others were out partying and dating he was building up his business, without any drama or distractions! He was financially healthy, with homes in London and France and his career now established. Another advantage he pointed out was being given a place at a top drama school at the age of 11, paid for by the local education authority, as he had been diagnosed a 'difficult' child. Without that label, he probably wouldn't have been able to go to this school, which he loved.

Gary has an attitude of gratitude that allows him to take something beneficial from his experiences. Another individual might well have chosen a different response, ending up bitter and angry, feeling blighted from the outset, betrayed by their own parents. As it is, he is one of the wisest, happiest, most uncomplicated individuals I've ever met – and great fun too!

Another man who has forged a remarkable life from unpromising beginnings is Ivan Massow. Ivan had three different surnames by the time he was 12, finally taking the name of his adoptive father. Severely dyslexic, he left school early with one qualification, in metalwork. Working in insurance in the 1980s, he saw how gay men were being penalised for their sexuality by insurers and went into business for himself, eventually making gay insurance a multimillion 'pink pound' business. He has run as an independent candidate for London mayor and would like to be a Tory MP. He has homes in London, Somerset and Ibiza.

Ivan Massow

> *I had a very difficult childhood. It involved care homes, foster parents and adoption. But it may well have a lot to do with why I do what I do. The added pressure of being dyslexic probably gave me the desire to set up a business. I felt stupid at school because all my friends would go into the top classes and I went into the bottom.*

I didn't have any qualifications and left school at 16. I could easily have ended up in prison. I was just a bit too smart really! I fell on the right side of the law by accident. I was offered jobs on building sites, in a butcher's shop or as an insurance clerk. I took the insurance job and did pretty well – I was an area manager at 21, company Peugeot and all that. It was the late 1980s, the height of the Aids scare, and the insurance industry was an incredibly homophobic industry. I would attend seminars where people would explain how to avoid giving gay men life insurance without being accused of discrimination. At the same time I was coming to terms with my own gay sexuality.

I had no idea how to run a business, but I wanted to try. I felt I had to do something about this. It felt like a crusade. I didn't know I was capable of success. I didn't know you could set up a business and make money. It was 1990, the beginning of deep recession, property prices were falling through the floor, interest rates at 15 per cent. People said no gay man would want to identify himself by coming to me for insurance. I came up against objection after objection, but I knew that it had to be done, and it would be important. So in 1990 I came to London, moved into a squat and launched the business from there. I couldn't take the risk of my housemates answering the phone to my potential customers, so I paid for an ultra-professional telephone answering service with a central London number. I always arranged meetings at smart restaurants to conceal the fact that there was no actual office. I wasn't bursting with confidence but I felt driven by a sort of pioneering spirit. I got round the difficulties and suddenly all these people who had been excluded could get insurance and mortgages.

The financial press made fun of my idea but thankfully it turned out to be a success. Six months after starting up, I was able to leave the squat, rent a flat in the smartest square in Islington and – buy a Ferrari! Well, I was 22. Within five years we had the tenth biggest turnover of any independent financial adviser in the UK. My latest venture, Massow Survivors, provides a service for another group that the insurance industry is reluctant to cover: survivors of cancer or major surgery, and those with mental health problems.

I'm proud of changing the insurance industry's view of gay people as consumers. When I started, insurance companies were taking the moral high ground by not insuring gay people; they were judging their lifestyle. It was a time when they were calling Aids 'God's plague'.

People sometimes attribute my success to dyslexia. There are four times as many dyslexics who are entrepreneurs than in the normal population – the same ratio as in prison. Our education system is unable to quantify that kind of intelligence, so dyslexics aren't able to survive in the education framework and have nothing to lose. It makes us natural risk takers. There is no one looking at us to see if we are going to fail, so we can take whatever risks we want.

I rarely equate success with money – although it can be a good marker. Money is not the driving force for me, it's boredom. I constantly reinvent myself out of boredom. What drives me is believing I can make a difference, that one person can make a difference, and constantly doing that. Everything I do is focused on moving things forward. My insurance company was a mission. It wasn't meant to be a business to make me rich, that happened by accident. After the death of my partner [James Knight, who committed suicide] I trained as a Samaritan. The training is useful for life and really teaches you how to deal with situations.

My business success pays for me to do other things. It fuels passions like the Prince's Trust. I talk to pre-release kids in the Feltham young offenders' unit about why they might have a propensity to entrepreneurship themselves. I point out how nicking car radios is, in a sense, entrepreneurial. I tell them we all fail but have to keep on trying – you could try not nicking car radios and apply your skills another way. I take any idea they have – however ridiculous it might sound – and show them how they could make it happen. They all come alive. They've never heard that before. They've just been told to pull themselves together and go and get a job at McDonald's. They're not acknowledged as people who are probably different in every way and are not likely to be good employees but might be great employers.

Fear of failure is the reason people stop succeeding. It's akin to fear of rejection. As you grow as a businessman you're scared of tarnishing your reputation. The higher up the ladder, the more you have to lose. You can start failing when you start succeeding because you've progressively got a reputation to lose. People take fewer risks, and often that leads to their decline. The only way out of that decline is to take risks again, so increasingly it's a cycle of failure and risk.

I'm in a hurry. I'm at a fork in the road and can do one of two major things, neither of which I may achieve. My sights are pretty high. They're political, and now I'm 36 I don't know whether I'm just going to fade away, or whether it's only the beginning. I just can't tell. I wake up every morning and invent every day completely from scratch. I'm going to keep on pushing and see what happens.

Ivan is utterly self-made. None of his early experiences or influences set him up to believe that he could make his own way in life, let alone be a millionaire, and the mover and shaker that he is. He has created his own self, is entirely self-determined. I was intrigued as to whether there was a particular instant when he had realised that his destiny was down to him. He replied, 'I think I just accepted at one point that I had nothing and no one to fall back on. I did feel let down by my parents and schools and knew that only I could make things happen for me. I really feel I was helped by that lack of support and I feel sorry for more privileged people with an education. They have so much to lose by mucking up.'

Notice how Ivan saw dyslexia as setting him apart and encouraging his entrepreneurial instincts: making him part of an elite four times more likely to be entrepreneurial than the 'normal' population. He's not wasting a drop of energy or focus in wishing he was 'normal'. There are no 'if onlys' in his outlook. He's too busy putting his advantages to work. He's glad to be different. Being unconventional also allowed him to bend a few rules and set up a business in a squat. Without the overheads of a formal office, or indeed a home, he was well positioned to make the business profitable from the outset. When he says that he kept on the right side of the law 'by accident', I disagree. It was no accident that he exercised his free will to determine which side of the track he would walk on. He might not have noticed at the time, but he was choosing all along, and the path of his life unfolded as a result.

Determine Yourself

Let's recap. I'm assuming that you're signed up to free will and self-determination and agree with me that self-belief is self-created. I've given you examples of individuals who shouldn't have strong self-belief, given their humble, even unpromising starts in life, yet have. I've given you the benefit of my anecdotal evidence demonstrating that we are all free to select self-belief, regardless of our origins. You will have your own examples to think about. You may have seen members of the same family choose entirely different responses to the same set of circumstances and influences. You will have seen rich people flounder and poor people prosper, defying the clichés about the best starts in life. You'll have seen individuals from 'good' homes end up in trouble and 'disadvantaged' kids succeed. Where's the sense in that?

The old advantages aren't the new advantages. The old ones may have been money and class. Those days are over. The new advantages are self-belief, passion, drive and self-determination.

No excuses, no looking back. Only forwards, knowing it's all down to you, knowing you have the talents, edge and advantages to make your life successful.

The writer and Green activist Julia Stephenson cuts an impressive figure. Beautiful, rich and talented, her life looks enviably perfect. But when I first met her, she appeared frail, tearful and suffered from stress-induced eczema. She had made the big break towards self-determination ten years earlier when she had initiated a divorce, a move from a country home to bachelor-girl London life and the writing of two successful novels inspired by her travels. She had also carved out a name for herself as a fearless Green campaigner, occasionally dismissed in the media as an 'eco-toff'. I admired her enormously because she could so easily have used her circumstances and wealth to complain that it had robbed her of her motivation to earn a living. Nor was she willing to drink, eat or medicate her way through life, another option open to her and favoured by many in her position.

Julia Stephenson

Although I was born into a wealthy background with every material comfort, family life was very unhappy. My parents' rocky marriage collapsed when I was seven years old, and from then on, home life was a nightmare.

These days it is usual to blame one's ghastly childhood for every misfortune in adulthood but I realised in my late twenties (all those wasted years!) that I just had to get over it and move on. Like many comfortably-off people, with time on my hands, I had done too much therapy. Now I can see it was a huge waste of time as it focused pointlessly on my gruesome childhood. All that did was make me sorry for myself, feel emotionally scarred and disabled, and resent my parents even more.

At 28 I was a housewife, stuck in an unhappy marriage and

living in a huge unwieldy concrete house in the Surrey countryside. I was frustrated and miserable. I longed to be a writer, but I really didn't believe that someone like me could ever publish a book. I lacked the courage and self-discipline even to try.

I had a private income, which is a wonderful advantage I am grateful for every day, but at that point in my life, I feel it may have taken away some of my motivation. I once heard a writer being interviewed, and when he was asked where he got his inspiration, he joked, 'Looking at my bank statement.' So although my motivation was not financial I was very powerfully driven by a need to prove myself, and I still am.

When I was at my lowest, my life began to change in the most extraordinary way after turning to Buddhism. I began to see that I was the only person who could improve it, firstly through a change in attitude and then through taking action. It was only when I decided what I wanted, set myself a seemingly impossible goal, and worked day by day towards realising it, that I began to create a positive momentum in my life. I started writing a novel, and I got divorced and returned to London.

Buddhism puts great emphasis on creating a happy family, and respecting one's parents no matter what. By focusing on my parents' many good points for the first time in my life, and developing a little more wisdom and compassion, my grudges began to dissolve. Consequently, our relationship has been transformed in a way I would never have believed possible. I learnt that replacing grudges with forgiveness and love is very freeing, and all areas of my life have continued to improve as a result.

Ten years later I have published two novels and also work lucratively as a freelance journalist, writing about subjects that interest me. I have represented the Green Party in Kensington and Chelsea in two general elections, and am active in the animal welfare world. While my family connections have proved helpful in opening doors, and providing publicity for my books, I hope that it is now my talent and determination that keep those doors open.

I remain constantly vigilant, for the crushing demons of self-doubt can easily return. In fact, two years ago I reached a rocky patch. My publisher and agent had lost interest in me writing a third novel. Vague attempts to kick-start my journalistic career had hit a brick wall. My occasional and tentative attempts to sell articles failed, leaving me utterly deflated. I used up huge amounts of nervous energy writing articles that were never published, mainly because I was too frightened to try to sell them. When I developed stress-related eczema I knew I had to do something. Talking to a life coach convinced me that I wasn't doing enough. So I forced myself to pick up the phone and talk to features editors. At first it was utterly terrifying. But I learnt that doing the terrifying thing is never as terrifying as you think it will be. And you feel fabulous afterwards.

Within a week of doing these very scary things, I had sold several articles. These were well received and I began to get commissions. Very soon, creative features ideas were gushing out of me. And from then on I was set on an upward spiral. The harder I worked, the luckier I got. New opportunities popped up. The BBC featured me in a television show where I was able to bring publicity to animal welfare charities and environmental concerns, and which also brought useful publicity for my books. I was on a roll.

My Buddhist practice, which is all about turning dreams into reality by taking hard, courageous, practical action was also incredibly important. An old proverb says that a block of marble is an obstacle to the weak and a stepping-stone for the happy. For many years all I could see were great slabs of marble blocking my progress, but fortunately I have switched my thinking around.

Free will can change something negative into something positive, or vice versa; it depends what we do with the circumstance. I was very lucky to discover that my mission in life was writing. I'm determined to use this talent not just to benefit myself, but

> *to repay the good fortune I am blessed with. I know from personal experience that the happiest, most fulfilled people are those who work altruistically to put something back.*

Julia's success is a direct result of her determination to exercise her free will and her awareness that self-belief requires constant reinforcement. She continues her political work, having stood for the Green Party in the 2005 general election, and is continually building her media work. Like her father before her, whose motivation was to make something of himself and run a successful business, Julia's is putting herself and her talents to good use to improve our world. Both are achieving their ends by the same self-determined perspective, looking only to themselves for their results and fulfilment.

We all want fulfilment, a feeling that what we do matters, that our lives are important and we are making our mark. Shaping and designing our lives so that we can fulfil our potential, express our talents and contribute to others is a human need, regardless of our bank balance. Julia grasped this challenge and began to transform her life with a change of mind, altering her attitude from passive and self-pitying to dynamic and pro-active. Think of your life as putty in your hands, waiting for you to shape it into the form you want it to take. Enjoy playing with the look and feel of it until it gets into a shape that inspires and motivates you.

The Secret of Self-belief

Who do you want to be? What beliefs do you want to have about *you*? Here's the secret to the quest for deep and lasting self-belief. You can choose to believe anything you want. That's the absolute truth. If you can first believe in this truth, you will have the key to your own soaring self-defined self-belief.

Don't confuse my simplicity with flippancy. Think about it. Whatever you believe to be true becomes rooted in your mindset as irrefutable. And whatever you believe sets your life on a particular course. You programme your direction from the parameters of your perspective. Nothing will change that course until you alter the settings, the programme. I saw this powerfully with a client who wanted to focus on her career, which she felt was not as successful as it might have been. Her romantic life, she said, needed no attention as she had always managed to attract any man she ever really wanted. I assure you she was not bragging, merely emphasising what she needed to work on to improve in her life.

On the premise that success in one area of your life can be analysed and lessons brought to other, less successful areas, I questioned Patricia on her attitude – and behaviour with men. What was the secret of her success? She acknowledged that she was no cover-girl Cindy Crawford, but perfectly pleasant and attractive in a wholesome, girl-next-door way. What emerged was that her belief that she was attractive to men was so strongly embedded in her make-up that it never occurred to her to even think about it: to question whether the man of her choice would find her attractive. She simply assumed that he would want to date her, proceeded to subtly let him know that she found him attractive and, hey presto, she always got her man! She never agonised over whether he would make his move, whether she was interesting enough, tall enough, small enough.

Her close relationship with her father undoubtedly helped as she had spent enormous amounts of time with him and grew up breathing in powerful messages about her personal worth. Be in no doubt that Patricia's success with men was a direct result of her thoughts and beliefs about herself in this arena. Her experience and reality served only to confirm her perspective. Had she ever suffered a setback or disappointment? Sure, but her take on that was remarkably philosophical, assuming that the man who let her down wasn't the guy she thought him to be and a better one would be along in good time.

In her professional life, though, Patricia felt none of the power and confidence that she did in her personal life. Her career was undemanding but unfulfilling. She ran a casting agency, finding photographers and models for fashion and advertising shoots. It sounds glamorous, but she longed to be a stylist but was too timid and unsure of her worth to promote herself, even though she already had good contacts in the industry. She had been 'styling' – putting together outfits, since she was four, and as her mother had been a dressmaker, she had learnt to make her own clothes at an early age. Patricia spent her spare time taking friends shopping for clothes and she was clearly gifted. She came to me at 32 knowing she had to do something about her lifelong passion.

I was intrigued to find out about her fail-safe strategy for romance, so that we could use it as a template for success in the career area of her life. She had a proven prescription for success and achievement, so it made sense to use it. Patricia had never really thought about what she did, but she knew that a train of events kicked in as soon as she spotted a prospective boyfriend! I asked her to talk me through exactly what she had done from the moment she spotted her current wonderful boyfriend. As I listened, I was able to pinpoint the precise mindset and methods that she followed. And, here it is:

1. Define the goal.

2. Continually visualise the successful outcome.

3. Be pro-active and create opportunities to be on the radar of the right people.

4. Anticipate a positive response, assuming people will be happy to see you or hear from you.

5. Be bold and imaginative in your approach to reach people and make progress.

6. Don't entertain self-doubt – have total regard for what you have to offer.

7. Feel excited as you look forward to your inevitable success!

Applying this approach over three months, Patricia built up a loyal client base of personal customers, worked on three shoots with an advertising agency, built up relationships with a number of key photographers, compiled an impressive portfolio, had been taken on by an agent and was on target to give up her full-time job. Oh – and she also got engaged to the wonderful boyfriend!

From your thoughts and beliefs springs your reality. From your ideas your future emerges. Your beliefs create your behaviour, and your behaviour creates your experience. What you believe, therefore, is crucially important. When I distilled Patricia's beliefs, they amounted to the very ones that I routinely use to help people adjust their mindsets in order to improve their relationship lives. Believing yourself to be attractive, seeing yourself as a catch, knowing what you bring to the party are all vital for success in attracting others. Some of us have to learn this, and unlearn our unhelpful beliefs. Others, like Patricia, don't have to give it a second thought.

You have more freedom to choose your beliefs about yourself than you may have ever appreciated. I have been in the business of building self-belief and increasing self-confidence for nearly twenty years. I have coached people to change their beliefs and self-belief and have seen at first hand the difference this makes to their entire lives. I have watched them make their dreams come true, fulfil their potential, live more interesting, exciting lives. Be assured, your self-belief is not fixed. You can double, quadruple your self-belief any time you like. Use the insights from the case studies in this chapter and the exercises below, all of which are based on my work with clients, and begin to create the self-belief you need to live the life of your dreams.

Build Self-belief from the Bottom Up

Firstly, we need to root out any beliefs that don't belong with you, that may belong to someone else's belief system, may be out-of-date or downright disastrous for you to be housing. It's best to clear out the old and create some space for new, more fitting and useful beliefs. Let's identify what has to go. Brainstorm through the following exercise before moving on to the next stage.

Out with the Old

1. A limiting belief I hold about myself is . . .
and another limiting belief I hold about myself is . . .
(write this out ten times and once for all subsequent answers)
Above all, my most limiting belief about myself is . . .

2. The effect of this belief on my life is . . .

3. This belief came from . . . and it stops me from doing . . .

4. A more productive belief I am replacing this with is . . .

5. If I really believed this, the difference it would make to my life is . . .

Creating Self-belief

I want you to isolate that most limiting belief you have owned up to and really look at from where and from whom it came. Most probably it has been there all your life and is so firmly embedded in your make-up that it's just a part of who you are, and feel, and see yourself to be. While it is interesting to pinpoint its source, it's important to understand that that entrenched belief has a vital part to play in your overall evolution because, as you confront and move beyond it, you're transforming yourself into an evermore refined version of you. These hurdles are nothing more and nothing less than opportunities for you to seize on the path to greater self-determination, self-belief and self-creation. If that path was smooth and straight, you'd have no obstacles to surmount and no feeling of euphoria as you leap and bound your way along. And a flat life would be downright dull.

Reject the temptation to resent the person or place that you feel this limiting belief may have come from. I don't want you to distract yourself from the main business of building yourself up and moving forwards. Additionally, if you accept my premise of free will, you'll agree with me that you invariably opted for this limitation at some point, for your own greater evolution. And, if you don't *agree* with me, assume with me, because it will take you in the direction you want to be going.

I want you to understand that this belief isn't true. It *has* been true because you've believed it to be so, operated from that premise and based your life on that 'truth'. You will have acquired a lifetime's worth of evidence to support its validity, attracting people and situations to reflect and confirm it for you. You've had faith in it.

This has to stop right here. From now on, you are conscientiously ungluing yourself from that nonsense. It no longer makes sense because you can see it for what it is, simply a belief that you took on board about yourself a very long time ago. Seeing this instantly distances you from it. For example, if you grew up believing yourself to be stupid, unattractive, boring or whatever, you'll know where that idea came from, and you'll know how it has affected you. Just because someone labelled you stupid doesn't mean it's true or that you have to continue to carry this label. Now is the time to question its foundation, dismiss its validity and begin your walk away from it.

Think about it. Twenty years ago you had beliefs that you don't have now. Some of these you might be embarrassed to remember, others are hilarious. I used to believe fervently, unequivocally, that only Catholics could get to heaven. Clearly, it would be a shame if I hadn't challenged that belief and replaced it with a more inclusive one! It's the same with a belief about yourself: you are no less free to laugh at it and turn your back on it, even if it did come from someone you once looked up to.

In the reconstruction of you, you must continually refute long-held beliefs that wreak havoc with your plans and aspirations. No belief can have authority over you unless you allow it to.

Dreaming the New

Before we get pragmatic, let's dream a little. Dreaming and scheming are both equally important in transforming self-belief. You have to excite yourself by thinking big before you set about making things happen. Give yourself a treat and take a moment to ask yourself: 'What would be fabulous to believe about me?'. 'What would be wonderful if it was really true?', and 'What belief would make a huge difference to my life if I really believed it to be true about me?'

Jot down a few of those beliefs. Don't worry if these questions feel a little repetitive. They're meant to be, so that you get to emphasise what's really important for you to begin to believe. Let's stay with the earlier example of the stupid belief. Let's say you identify that believing that you are smart as opposed to stupid would be fabulous and would make a huge difference to your life. Get a taste for feeling smart. Is it wonderful? Good. Now let's begin to make it real for you and easier to believe. You have already questioned the validity of your old belief that you were stupid. Now, look for evidence to show you are smart, and by that I don't just mean narrow academic smartness. So, you weren't a swot? So, where did your smartness show up? I want you to look for the evidence that proves your new belief. It's there. You may not have noticed before, because you were so focused on believing the opposite. As the best-selling self-help author Wayne Dyer says, 'You are what you think about all day long.' If you were busy thinking 'I'm stupid', then that's how you will have seen yourself. You were like a heat-seeking missile, looking for what you had been programmed to look for. If Ivan Massow had been looking for smartness in the conventional academic sense, he'd have been in trouble. Luckily, he was clever enough to look beyond this definition to spot his own smartness.

You must do the same with your new understanding and definition of you. Look for the evidence in your life that justifies your new thinking about yourself. The more rooted in 'reality' your new-found beliefs are, the easier and quicker you'll accept them and take them to heart. You are the person who needs convincing. Once you are convinced, you'll convey your conviction to others, who, as always, will reflect back to you your most strongly felt beliefs. Make your new beliefs as believable as possible by justifying their authenticity to yourself. You need reasons to switch allegiance from one belief to another. Focus on that new belief and begin a list headed, 'Evidence that *already* exists in my life to show this is true'. You will be amazed to see how quickly you can convince yourself of your new position when you see the proof that you're looking for. Keep this list open until you are utterly convinced. For example, evidence of your smartness might include running the family budget or being the first person friends turn to for guidance in a crisis.

So, *you* decide what it's to be that you believe. Become very choosy about what you choose to believe. Select your beliefs carefully. Guard your thoughts, as they are the route to your belief system. We know that our thought patterns tend to be repetitive, so repeat only that which is useful for you to believe. Call it affirmation or conscious thinking, but get a handle on the fact that what you're telling yourself is true. As Disraeli said more than 150 years ago, 'Nurture your mind with great thoughts, for you will never go any higher than you think.'

Be Able to Justify Your Beliefs

I am assuming you are a sane, rational person and that the beliefs you are selecting for yourself are in keeping with an uplifting, expansive direction for you. Additionally, to anchor your beliefs in your life, you do have to be able to justify them to yourself and, often, to others too.

I saw an excellent example of unjustified self-belief recently on a television makeover programme. In *Kitchen Nightmares*, Michelin-starred chef Gordon Ramsay visited a failing restaurant to discover why it was doing so badly. The culprit was in the kitchen – an arrogant young chef who was offering complex *haute cuisine* menus when he hadn't mastered the knack of cooking a decent omelette. He boasted about his ambitions to run restaurants of his own, blaming his lack of customers on the lack of sophisticated people in the neighbourhood. His bravado was hilarious but was rapidly dragging the business towards bankruptcy (which was what eventually happened). The fact that his kitchen was also filthy sabotaged any sympathy we might have had for him.

What should this young chef have done? He should have ensured that his self-belief was justified. His skills should have been honed to perfection, either by working as an apprentice to masters like Ramsay, or he should have put himself through the best possible formal training, especially as he hadn't grown up in a gastronomic home. Cooking may well have been his passion but he was not respecting that love by ensuring he was as brilliant at it as he made himself out to be. Now, this is the sort of person who gives self-belief a bad name!

A rather different young man who was unfairly called arrogant for his self-belief and ambitious plans was Roger Bannister. Fifty years ago he achieved one of the most notable sporting feats of all time, becoming the first man to run a mile in under four minutes. At the time this was believed to be impossible for mere mortals and doctors warned that the heart and lungs could explode with the strain. The press vilified him for his supposed conceit but he was desperate to prove himself. On a cold and windy day, on an obscure track in Oxford in front of just 1,500 people, Bannister pulled off one of sport's magic moments. He left nothing to chance in making himself the best in the world, having trained himself mentally and physically for this triumph all his life. Unshakeable self-belief, justified by evidence, honoured by action, is the way to go.

The last of our case studies in this chapter demonstrates that mantra perfectly. Simon Woodroffe has worked as a roadie, lighting engineer, stage-set designer for rock groups and media salesman. At 40 he felt that he had never reached his potential and time was ticking away. One day a Japanese acquaintance said, 'What you should do, Simon, is start a conveyor-belt sushi bar.' Simon launched Yo! Sushi in London's Soho in February 1997 with the banner headline, 'World's Largest Conveyor-Belt Sushi Bar' when there were only a handful of such places outside Japan. Knowing nothing about restaurants and not a lot about sushi,

Simon went on to win Emerging Entrepreneur of the Year 1999 and UK Group Restaurateur of the Year 2000. Yo! Sushi now has twenty branches in the UK, franchises in Dubai and Athens, and turnover for 2005 is on target to exceed £16 million. In 2006, Simon launches his futuristic hotel concept, Yotel, at all major UK airports.

Simon Woodroffe

When I started as an entrepreneur, I got out of bed at four in the morning many, many times because of a passion for what I was doing and the fear of failure. One of the things that I've always done, and it's not a new and original thought, is step out of my comfort zone. When I put myself on the line, whether it's by signing a contract or by telling someone I'm going to do something, then I actually fight my way through the problem because I don't want to fail. I have just signed a contract with a promoter to do a one-man show at the Edinburgh Festival for twenty-three consecutive days in August and I don't yet know what that show is going to be.

When I reached 40 I could envisage myself becoming a bitter old man and resentful that I hadn't done any of the things I felt enthusiastic and passionate about. Before I started Yo! Sushi I researched lots of different ideas. That was probably a really big driver, together with the fact that I didn't have a great income at the time and I had quite a few commitments. The thought of working for somebody else was so dire that I had to do something. I think very often if you get to that age and you haven't fulfilled your potential and your career is muddled or has gone wrong, but you have lots of experience, especially of failure, you're extremely investable. I would put my bet on someone like that because there's a very big desire to succeed.

After I got over the euphoria of starting Yo! Sushi, a little voice in the back of my head kept saying, 'If this was such a good idea, someone who knew a lot more about restaurants than me would have done it a long time ago.' I could have stopped at that stage, but the more research I did, the more I realised that it needed somebody who wasn't a restaurateur to carry out the idea. Sometimes going into a business that you don't have any experience of is an advantage, especially in this changing world, because you can see things differently.

I had a hint of self-belief at 40 and once I got going on a good project that gave me confidence. Confidence is a very interesting thing. When you don't feel confident, it's almost impossible to imagine what it actually feels like to act and be confident on a day-by-day basis. In Japan, they don't have a word for good luck, but their equivalent phrase is Keep going. *You can get bogged down by little problems and details but if you've got a longer-term vision that isn't hooked into whether you do a project or not, but is just researching it, then you've always got that to fall back on.*

My dad, who was a very risk-averse senior army officer, said 99 per cent of businesses fail and I probably would have listened to him if I'd had some qualifications. I didn't, so I didn't have a choice. After leaving school, I wanted to buy a transit van to take people on the hippie trail to India. My main motivation was to make money from doing it. My mum was from a semi-aristocratic family but in the world we came from, we were always less well off than others. I remember my dad would buy a bottle of gin from the supermarket and he wouldn't like it to be known that he didn't buy it by the case. As I was growing up, I always felt a bit less than people around me and I compensated for that by acting rather big, and I probably still do it today. My brother has done very well as a lighting designer, working for the Rolling Stones *and all sorts of people, and he's very, very well respected in his field.*

My parents got divorced and it wasn't that stable a family, so I really cocked up at school and left at 16. That's had two influences on me: one is that with no qualifications to fall back on you have to rely on yourself, so your brain is always scheming, first of all in the early days just to survive. It also meant that from a fairly young age, I learnt to deal with a great deal of insecurity and a great deal of pain. Once you've done that and realised that it's not going to kill you, you're willing to take risks because you realise that when the emotional pain of taking them comes up, you can cope with it.

The second thing about not going through A-levels and a university education is I don't have a trained mind, so I'm not good at concentrating over long periods and dealing with the complex analysis of situations. I can pick things up instinctively and I get a gut feeling and then I make a decision. By not having a formal education, the imagination that is inherent in children when they grow up wasn't drummed out of me. When I have an idea, I ban my brain from deciding whether I'm going to do something or not. My job is to put some time and money into doing research and then I make the decision at the end. I'm always trying to put my energy into doing the right things in the right order and making the right next move, rather than worrying about the outcome.

I am happier than I have ever been and I'm very proud of what I've achieved. However, after running Yo! Sushi for the first three years, I handed the reins over to our operations director and he ran the company how he wanted. Things went down at the very beginning but then they came up way beyond what I could have done. This taught me that empowering other people is really the way to build a large organisation, which is what I'm trying to do.

Now all the new ventures that I'm setting up have other people in charge. My strategy is not to sit at the top of the pyramid but to have a licence with the companies that we're involved with. I take a minority share and we protect the brand. The day-to-day anxiety is therefore reduced and I can look at the bigger picture.

> *The future for me is trying to build a brand called Yo! with a group of people involved in running it who are like-minded, kindred spirits. A brand needs to reflect the people who created it. Being part of the world we live in, and contributing to that, is every bit as important as the shareholders' returns. A magical thing can happen when you have that sort of attitude in a business, causing returns to improve because clients and the people who work within companies think alike. In the twenty-first century, what you stand for is every bit as important as what you sell.*

The lasting impression I have of Simon is of a man hell-bent on fulfilling his potential. As I waited to speak to him at the Yo! HQ in London, he was finishing a call about his show at the Edinburgh Fringe Festival, *How I Got My Yo!* When I asked him what he would do over those twenty-three evenings he admitted that he had no idea. It was obvious that scaring himself into action and running the risk of failure keep him living right on the edge of his potential. And not every risk has paid off. He struggled to get Yo! into the Millennium Dome, which was hardly a success, and lent the Yo! name to a horrible range of pre-packed supermarket sushi.

That's not to say he takes his risks lightly. Before his one-man show I heard that he had hired a top director, singing teacher and movement teacher, giving him every chance of success. I had the feeling that performing and entertaining were a lifetime's dream he could now afford to fulfil, in his own way. He could afford to hang out and enjoy his wealth and fame, but he is entranced by the notion of pushing himself to see what else he can do, where his limits are and how to go beyond them. On the day before his opening night at Edinburgh I read an interview he gave in *The Times* where he said, 'You have to embarrass yourself in front of people, be rejected. If you're able to do that and not take to heart what other people say, then you can do anything.' Now that's what I call self-belief.

Five Steps for Greater Self-belief

1. Embolden yourself. Take on a project that will expand your self-belief. If you didn't take on the mission suggested at the end of the last chapter, do it now. Your project should allow you to feel passionate, fulfil your purpose, incorporate your strengths, stretch your self-belief and achieve your potential.

2. Encourage yourself. Praise and reward are more useful to you than criticism and punishment. Fuel your growing self-belief with loving kindness. Keep your spirit strong and your resolve steady with the right backing.

3. Choose self-determination. The past is over. Your childhood is over. You're free to choose what to believe and who to be. It's all down to you. Watch your thinking as it's shaping your life.

4. Appreciate your advantages. Never forget how fortunate you are, whatever your story. Ensure you make full use of the edge it gives you. Do you feel lucky? You should do.

5. Select a guiding belief. What belief provides the strongest motivation for your life? Keep that belief by your side. Let this be your mantra, for all the good times and the more challenging ones too!

3: *Do* MORE!

It was Albert Einstein who observed, 'Nothing happens until something moves.' He may have been talking about quantum physics and the movement of energy, but that's the essence of our next rule, **Do More!** If there's one rule that all the achievers in this book share, it's this one: they're all doers. They do more than the average person. And because this rule is so glaringly obvious, it's often overlooked in our quest to discover some hidden recipe for success in life and the secret of others' success. Here's the blinding truth that I came face to face with in the making of this book: successful people *do more* than their less successful counterparts.

I know there may be spiritual masters down the ages who only have to think of their desires and hey presto, they materialise out of the ether for them. The rest of us have to put the work in to get the same results. Look at every single person who impresses you with their accomplishments and you'll see a man or a woman of action. Less talk, far more action.

A Woman of Action

I'll never forget an interview I read more than ten years ago with the phenomenonal Tina Brown, dubbed 'the Queen of New York' well before she was 40, not bad for an Englishwoman. She turned around *Vanity Fair* and then the *New Yorker*, making them essential reading in a country with thousands of magazines. In professional circles she is known as the most formidable editor in the world. This interview was carried out in 1993 when she was editing the *New Yorker*, which was then the smartest magazine in the West. Take a look at her attitude:

> I turn from one thing to the next and I work very hard and I think about it all the time: isn't that what everyone does? In order to sustain a job like mine and make it work you've got to be tremendously focused. I don't have much leisure. I think about the magazine all the time, twenty-four hours a day, in the car, in the bath: all the time. It's a very fascinating and consuming and rewarding job. I love my job. I love my life.

Now look at her normal daily routine:

> I get up at 5.45 and go to the gym at the end of the street for an hour. I never used to do that, but I really find it gets me through the day and gives me energy. Then I have my shower, wake my children up, walk Isabel [her daughter] to the International Free School and come to work. I try not to leave work after 5.30, and then, between 6 and 9 p.m. it's bedlam with the children. Finally George [her son] goes to bed and then it's like 'The Elves and the Shoemaker' because I do a lot of work in the evenings at home: the faxes begin, and it's another sort of bedlam. I sleep less than six hours a night which I truly don't like, but I need that little to spend any time with my children.

You may shy away from a routine like that, but at least you're in no doubt about the sheer level of activity that a hugely successful individual such as Tina Brown puts in to produce the results she achieves. I am reminded of something another great achiever, Thomas Edison, once said: 'Genius is one per cent inspiration, and ninety-nine per cent perspiration.' How often do you sweat?

Courage vs. Confidence

At the risk of sounding controversial, one of the biggest problems with some self-improvers is that they don't grasp this basic rule; they just don't *do more*. They read, they talk and they take too many courses, when all that time and energy, and probably money too, could be better spent in doing the things they know they should be getting on with. My intention with *The 7 Rules of Success* is that you can pick up valuable information and tips in these pages and apply what you find useful to your life immediately.

Another pitfall to watch out for is that of waiting to feel more confident before making a move: 'working' on your self-belief before you feel up to making a call, offering a service, writing your novel, setting up a business or whatever you feel pulled to do. Don't make this mistake. Forget about confidence for a while and substitute courage instead. Assume with me – because it's probably true – that *everyone* feels inadequate and unsure at the outset of a new venture. To use that uncertainty as a reason to hesitate, or even abandon your plan, would be most unwise. The trick is to accept this state as entirely par for the course and carry on regardless. Attempting to 'work' on your confidence before taking action can often be a waste of time because the confidence you crave can only come from doing the very thing you are terrified of. Shakespeare put it well when he said, 'Our doubts are traitors, and make us lose the good we oft might win by fearing to attempt.' Slay your doubts and demons with good old-fashioned action.

Often, necessity is the mother of inspired action. This was certainly the case with Trisha Mason. Her success, by her own admission, was born partly from tragedy. Back in the spring of

1975, Trisha was a 29-year-old widow, living in a dilapidated east London home with two young children, Kate and Jake, with no savings, no earnings, and bills to pay. Just five months earlier, she and her husband Julian had been preparing for Christmas and making plans for renovating the Victorian terrace house in Leytonstone they had bought for £12,000. But when Julian, a 32-year-old university electronics engineer, began to suffer from back pains, medical tests diagnosed a cancer so virulent that he died the next April.

Worried about how she was going to cope as a single mother, Trisha turned herself into a powerhouse of activity in order to keep a roof over their heads and give her kids a good life. Her story is no fairy tale, just an example of one woman drawing on every talent and ability she could find within herself to make life work. It wasn't even about something as lofty as fulfilling her potential. That would have been a luxury she could ill afford. It was just about doing what had to be done, under the circumstances.

Trisha Mason is the founder of one of the most successful estate agencies in France. With a £3–5 million turnover in 2005 and 10,000 French properties sold to English buyers to date, the company now has around thirty offices in France run by specially trained English staff. Trisha's loss forced her to develop an entrepreneurial spirit that has led to her present success and a company that has been voted Best French Estate Agents three times in the International Property Awards.

Trisha Mason

When my husband died suddenly of cancer, leaving me with two small children, Gingerbread (a single-parent action group) sent someone I considered ancient round to talk to me. She said, 'I guess you find yourself drinking an awful lot of tea. Too many cups of tea isn't good for you, dear.' I thought, I don't want to be labelled as drinking too much tea. Too much gin, fine, but not too much tea! And strangely enough, that had an awful lot to do with my desire to achieve. Her comment made me face what my two options were. I could either accept tea and sympathy or aim for the high life and drink the gin and tonic in the evenings.

I was left with my grief, a rotten old house and no income. I've always loved challenges and it was a case of needs must that I had to earn money – but I also relished the fight.

My husband and I had hippie idealism ingrained in us from the 1960s and that certainly didn't mean existing on the state. We were never materialistic but we did have a common dream about how we wanted our children's lives to be. It meant having adequate money to take them travelling and continue those dreams. I guess I felt I owed it to him. I was always driven to do more. When my husband died, I was working in a mental hospital trying to establish a toy library for adult patients. I used to take my children along with me. We always did everything very much as a family, which was why I felt my only option was to set up my own business so they could be with me.

My husband had been working in a low-salaried job and we had no savings, no pension, nothing except a big four-bedroom house that was falling down around our ears. What I did have was plenty of friends. We used to sit around my kitchen table drinking wine, rather than tea I might add, and they actually came up with the first business idea for me. I'd always liked making my children clothes that were different from everyone else's. They suggested I make similar clothing and they'd go and sell them at the markets for me. So I started making clothes and ended up setting up a company called 'Country Bumpkins'. I spent my time with the kids during the day and then at 8 p.m., once I'd put them to bed, a rota of friends would come over and we'd work until about 2 a.m. We very quickly realised we weren't going to maximise our potential at the markets so we took samples to various retail outlets.

Almost immediately we got orders from Harrods, Selfridges and Harvey Nichols and a business was created. It was a great business. The children were my models. We had a small factory opposite the nearest tube station to where we lived, so after school they'd come in, sweep the floor, make covered buttons, etc. They've always been part of everything I've done and both still work in my current company. That lasted about ten years. The end of the 1980s hit us badly when interest rates soared. Shops stopped holding stock themselves and expected manufacturers to instead.

We simply didn't have enough capital to do that so we sold off everything and came out of it with nothing – but I did have ten years' experience under my belt. By that time my daughter was about to do her A-levels and my son, his GCSEs. At the time my husband died, I was doing an Open University course in law. Through our local vicar, I was introduced to someone who needed help with his own businesses. I ended up running indoor market halls, car hire firms and industrial estates while studying for my degree!

In the year of my finals, the children and I went off as usual on our annual month's holiday to France. Whilst out there, I found a beautiful mill in the Limousin that I simply fell in love with. I tried to get a mortgage without really thinking about why I was doing it; I just thought it would be lovely for my children to spend their summer holidays there and have it as their second home. Almost immediately, friends and family came to visit and wanted me to find them something similar.

After six or seven requests, I realised there was a business to be created here and consequently, that became business number two. It was a risk but I started to take a small exhibition space when overseas property exhibitions were only just beginning in the UK. At that time, seventeen years ago, estate agents in France didn't really exist, so I was relying on our village solicitor who dealt with the local real estate to inform me of any properties that came up in the area. For the first three years, I would meet people at Dover, drive them to central France, find them a house and then drive them back to England again. By then, I'd realised that this was going to be a good business so in 1987 I sold the London house and bought a small flat in Docklands, which at that time was incredibly cheap because nobody wanted to live there. And the rest of the money went into making my business grow.

My French back then was very basic, but I thought I could offer my experiences of buying a property from scratch. I started out working at the kitchen table and it was all a bit ad hoc, with business papers strewn all around and me answering the phone while cooking supper. I put in a huge effort, cooking for clients and taking them around the area and to view houses. I'd often work late into the evening with a pen in one hand and a glass of wine in the other. I loved the challenge. It was very much a case of learning on the job, but I loved every minute of it so there was no hardship involved. I knew I was on to something when I received so many inquiries through word of mouth.

People live on in the actions they inspire in you by their death. Within two years of losing my husband, I understood that his gift to me was the strength to take risks. I realised that even though I'd lost the one person that mattered most to me in the world, I had still survived.

I now have over 150 people working for my business. My team is growing up professionally and in terms of their knowledge of the business. I've committed myself to another eighteen months of full-time work. I know I've got another project in me though. I'd really like to give something back to the world. It'll probably be something where I can use my skills to help really disadvantaged people who haven't been blessed with my energy, if nothing else. I was born into a working-class family. It's a case of helping people to make a change in their lives and to understand how they can affect what happens to them. I want to give people the life skills to create the right environment for themselves in which they can flourish.

Keeping on and keeping going is vital. I've had a lot of setbacks, particularly in this current business because I was at the forefront of anybody trying to work within Europe. I often felt like giving up but my friends persuaded me to stick in there – I remember a friend once sending me a packet of perseverance seeds. I received a card from another friend recently which said: To my best friend – who is able to turn everything to her good fortune and then share it with everyone she loves.

Today, there is so much interest from Britain that Trisha has opened offices in Charente, Limousin's neighbouring region, Brittany and Normandy, and is about to expand into Spain and Italy. You can't help but admire the woman's spirit! From a truly bleak situation she forced herself to face her choices and took the decision to make her life work, especially for her two young children. It would have been easy to be swallowed up by self-pity and sympathy, but as she says herself, that just wasn't a route she was prepared to take. There are no secrets to Trisha's success. Her strategy is blatantly simple and available to all of us: action and more action. Serendipity and good fortune played their part along the way, but only when she was already out on the road, making things happen. It never occurred to Trisha to query whether she was 'qualified' to do any of the jobs she did or the two businesses she created: 'learn as you go' was her approach. Additionally, there was no great soul-searching as to what her next move should be when 'Country Bumpkins' came to an end: the French property company was born from her falling in love with a run-down mill while on holiday in France. There's probably some truth in the saying that life happens when you're busy making other plans!

That was certainly the case with Eamonn Holmes. One of five boys from a Northern Irish working-class family, Eamonn had a grammar-school education and trained to be a bartender. He worked in a bar in Belfast at the same time as presenting the sports news on television in Northern Ireland. Nowadays he is one of the country's most popular and sought after television presenters. For twelve years he was the anchorman for GMTV's morning news programme. He left in May 2005 and less than six months later, Eamonn relaunched Sky's breakfast news programme *Sunrise* for a deal reported to be worth £2.8 million.

Eamonn Holmes

I started out wanting to be a news reporter, became a sports reporter and ended up quiz/chat show host! It wasn't something I had ever intended to do. But this is the only way I know how to make my living.

So many people in broadcasting are motivated by celebrity or fame. I'm lucky that hasn't really played a huge part for me. I just wanted to be a reporter. As it turned out, you can rarely be master of your own destiny once you enter the world of TV. It's like the Grand National – there are so many runners, so many fences and so many fallers. The skill is to last the course. So many people would pay to get into this business. But I just want to do the job well. I'm not complacent about losing it all as I've now got a lot of responsibilities. The key art is to adapt and to be multi-media. I'm also very lucky that I work in something I have a passion for. It can be a very superficial business, though. If you are blessed with incredibly good looks, you get maybe five years out of this business – so if you can build a career without looks, it should be longer!

What I have is a fantasy job. I always thought I'd be a barman. When I was 15, my dad got me and my younger brother a job in a bar and I learnt to get on with all sorts of people and do the job to the best of my ability. I worked there until I was 21. By 1982, and still working in the bar in the evening, I had started to appear on the teatime TV sports desk on Ulster television.

My father was a carpet fitter; he knew everyone from judges to bin men. He loved talking and meeting people and they loved talking to him. He carried on working until he died at 65. His great skill was that he made people laugh. He was such a character – two thousand people came to his funeral because he was a man people liked.

Like my dad, who made his job look easy though it wasn't, I worked very hard at knowing all aspects of what I had to do; learning to write as I speak, for example. You can't write for television as you would as a print journalist. There's a knack to the naturalness of broadcasting. Once I'd learnt the technicalities, I made it look as easy as I could. The people who broadcast well don't need to put mystique around it.

But as with most things in life, the line between succeeding and failing can be very, very thin. When I started out at BBC Manchester, I thought I was pretty good at what I did, but when a new boss came in, I lost my job after five years – was in huge debt, had to sell my car, and my family had to move back to Belfast where it was cheaper to live. Thankfully, I don't have an ego with regards to work so I rolled up my sleeves and got £45 per shift at the BBC in London.

From 1990 to 1993, I took everything going. I used to do a reporting shift, come back and edit into the night, grab a couple of hours' sleep at a desk and then I'd brush my teeth, shave and start another shift presenting the sport on BBC Breakfast News. Since I was away from my family anyway I thought that was a very good use of my time. I was doing very well on the sports desk and was also presenting the Holiday Programme*, which paid me a measly £250 per week for ten weeks. That £2,500 was then taxed and agent's fees deducted which meant I became completely broke. This career I knew I was privileged to have was nonetheless putting me in further debt. I was* *getting high profile and brand but no money. It was only by putting in the extra hours that I was keeping my head above water. So I resolved not to work in the media unless I was paid the money I felt I deserved. I could see that I was better than most and now was the time to get paid more than most.*

I would have been happy to go and clean cars, cut grass, go back to the bar. I didn't need to be well known and hard up. I just needed money to support my growing family responsibilities. I remember going to GMTV in 1992. I should have been grateful to join them, but I was determined this would be a deal based on finance rather than fame. Happily, as a result they paid me £90,000 to join them! Even better, I was free to work for other people as well. But after only six weeks presenting sport on a Sunday, I was pulled off the subs bench because the other presenting team didn't work out and I was put on the main show. I had learnt always to negotiate when you are most needed. So, they upped my salary to £120,000 and I was finally off and running.

Absolutely no one pushes me about. I watched my father doing his job and it was always the well-off people who would try to short-change him, rarely those who were short of a few bob. I remember just before he died, these big-business men refused to pay the full amount for work he had carried out. He was tearful about it. He said that was how they had so much money – because they don't give it away. I'm a great believer in always giving people their dignity. I've always been involved with trade unions and business with a conscience. If only everyone was the same, but there are a lot of bad guys out there. The number of people over the years who have tried to diddle me or have thought they could get away with bullying me, is unbelievable. That's why my dad and John Wayne are my great influences – things are either bad or good, black or white and you stand up for the weak and those who can't do it for themselves. I stand up to bullying and against tyranical bosses. I can name lots of people above me I have stood up to but never one person beneath me.

I would like to be lazy but I work huge hours – eighteen to twenty a day. I do all different types of television: sport, news, current affairs, chat shows, quiz shows. I'm lucky that I'm accepted for having a range of skills. I write for newspapers and also do radio. I'm certainly not addicted to work, but much of it is strategic. In the freelance market, having one job often leads to another. I do like money, though; I spend it and am generous with it. I'm very driven to provide for my children and those around me.

I have always been a fan of Eamonn Holmes, not just because he's a brilliant presenter but because we're both products of the same working-class, Northern Irish background. We both passed the eleven-plus and went to Catholic grammar schools: he was taught by priests while I had the Sisters of Mercy! For Northern Irish Catholics, this was enormously significant, the route to bettering ourselves and a good life. One of the things that stands out with Eamonn's story is his willingness to do almost *anything* to earn a living, to take care of his family and stay in work. And while he was busy taking action, staying busy, his big break with GMTV came. Ironically, it was this experience that has helped make him one of the most versatile and professional presenters in television today. He proves Woody Allen's point that 95 per cent of success is showing up!

In the showbiz world he now inhabits, he's never lost sight of who he really is and why he's working and what's really important. When we met to discuss all this, he arrived late and fuming that his taxi driver had just been given a parking ticket for pausing and chatting to Eamonn as he dropped him off outside the restaurant. And, even though he had been up since 4 a.m. at GMTV and wouldn't get to bed before midnight after presenting the *National Lottery* show, there wasn't a shred of self-importance or impatience about him. Ever the professional, his main concern was whether my tape recorder needed new batteries and whether we should move to a quieter corner to get a better sound quality! Now that's a man who cares about doing a job properly.

Action and Attraction

You're probably familiar with the saying, 'If you want something done, ask a busy person.' I find that a really interesting notion. A busy person is already in the habit of getting things done, making things happen. There's a momentum, perhaps urgency to the way in which they conduct themselves. There's an edge to them, dynamism, energy. All of which is very attractive, and we're naturally drawn towards individuals like these. They're magnetic, compelling. As I see it, there are distinct advantages to being a busy person. Firstly, you're visible. You show up on the radar. People see you and think of you when jobs and contracts are being dealt out. Even if you're not doing the thing you really want to be doing, you stand a better chance of discovering what that is while you're out there doing *something*, and you'll come across more people, possibilities and opportunities than you would tucked away at home. When Eamonn Holmes got his big break with breakfast television, there was no missing him. He was everywhere.

Secondly, busy people already have an air of success around them. They're in demand, already in the flow. They're sought after, or it certainly looks that way, and if we have to go on a waiting list to see them, so much the better.

It's also true that divine providence and serendipity, good luck and fortuitous coincidences only kick in when you're already out there, sowing seeds and ploughing your own furrow. They don't seek you out behind closed doors, preferring to meet you halfway. You have to get out and about to have any chance of meeting them.

Finally, as a busy person, you're more likely to be stretching and developing yourself, striving to achieve and succeed rather than waiting for life to come to you. Therefore, you're invariably growing into a far smarter, more resourceful version of yourself. I think this is what John F. Kennedy was getting at when he explained his goal to 'put a man on the moon and safely return him to earth by the end of the decade'. This was how he put it: 'But why, some say, the moon? Why choose this as our goal . . . ? We choose to go to the moon in this decade and do the other things, not because they are easy, but because they are hard. Because that goal will serve to organise and measure the best of our energies and skills.'

So, the message is, bite off more than you can chew and chew like mad! As living legend and Hollywood screen-writing guru Robert McKee says, 'If you want to die happy, get off your ass and do something before the freight train arrives.'

This is exactly what Tamara Hill-Norton did when she opened her first shop, Sweaty Betty. With no great retail or business expertise she raised money from friends, family and the bank to back her hunch that women would welcome stylish fitness and leisurewear. That was eight years ago and since then she's turned her company into the UK's leading women's sportswear chain. There are eleven outlets in London, others in Brighton and Bristol and another twenty planned to open throughout the UK by 2006. Tamara is married to Simon and has two daughters, Honor, two, and Daisy, four.

Tamara Hill-Norton

It wasn't until I was at university, studying languages, that it slowly dawned on me what I should do with my life. While I was on my year abroad I came up with the idea that I wanted to set up my own underwear business. I was living in France and there was such beautiful underwear on sale and it really inspired me. Looking around, wondering what to do after university, I thought a mail-order underwear catalogue would be a good idea. So I applied to Knickerbox, the underwear chain, and it was when I was working there that I came up with the idea of doing sportswear. It seemed to me there was a real niche in the market.

From my own experience, I also knew it was a good idea. I love shopping but I could never find decent sports and leisurewear and I discovered there were lots of other women who were in the same position. One of the manufacturers I was dealing with at Knickerbox had just started manufacturing 'USA Pro', a new brand designed in England specifically for women. All the other sports brands I'd come across were primarily for men with women's sportswear basically just scaled-down versions of men's. I looked at this fantastic catalogue and I thought, Wow! That was enough to get me really excited.

I had already started to write a business plan when Knickerbox went bust and I was made redundant. In retrospect, that was incredibly useful because it finally gave me the kick up the backside to stop talking about what I'd always dreamt of doing and just do it – open my own sports and leisurewear shop exclusively for women. I was by now married to Simon and so I had a bit of a cushion. If I hadn't been in that situation I would have just had to do it differently. I would have had to work and find the time from somewhere to write my business plan. But I would have found a way to do it.

Not really knowing how to go about setting up a business was a really big help in a way because I didn't know the pitfalls. But I did have Simon, who was incredibly supportive and has a lot of business acumen. He helped me to hone the business plan over six months and when we had it finished, we went to friends and family and said, 'Look, we've got this crazy idea, how do you fancy giving us £5,000?' We managed to raise £60,000 to start with, mostly from friends and family but with a little bit of bank debt as well, and that was enough to secure the first shop. I think people took the risk assuming that the two of us together couldn't really go that wrong. But the process of justifying the plan was a bit maddening. I had so much faith in the idea that I struggled with having to sell it to potentially sceptical investors. Since then I've raised finance four times and had to justify it every time.

Securing the first shop was an absolute nightmare. That really was the worst part of the whole process for two reasons. It's difficult to get a landlord to take anyone on without previous experience and as the shop had gone into administration it was a really horrible legal upheaval. Notting Hill was becoming very trendy, but it was still a bit of an unknown. The property was in a really dodgy little block, with a pawnbroker's on one side and a 7/11 corner shop on the other. The pawnbroker told us they had had a stabbing in the shop two months earlier, and the area was constantly threatened by gangs who were after labels like Nike and Adidas. When he heard that I was opening a sportswear shop staffed by women he told me I was absolutely mad. So it was quite a scary prospect but I just thought, It has to be the right thing to do. I could see our target customers were already living and shopping in the area.

We were hoping to open in March 1998 and we didn't actually open until November. This was disastrous because the way that clothing retail works is you have to order stock six months in advance, which I did, so all this stock started arriving at our home. It had been so difficult getting all these brands to agree to supply us, particularly Nike and Adidas, that there was absolutely no way I could ring them up and say, 'Look, I can't take the stock now. I don't have a shop.' So it just kept coming in, piling into our home. It was a really horrible time and I think I lost about a stone and a half in weight.

I was really, really stressed but I never once thought of giving up. I simply knew it was going to work. I had this unerring feeling that we were doing the right thing. Within two weeks of opening there was a great article on us in the Evening Standard. *That publicity launched us. It literally put us on the map. After all we'd been through it was an absolutely amazing feeling.*

It wasn't all glorious to start with, though. I had one other girl working with me. She was totally inexperienced and with Christmas two weeks away she resigned, leaving me on my own in the shop. I was working seven days a week, twelve hours a day, if not more. Every time the shop alarm went off in the middle of the night, I was up there in my car. But it was my baby and I loved it. I identify really strongly with our customers and genuinely love our products.

When we wrote the business plan I learnt one important thing: you're not going to attract investors if you just do it for a hobby because they want to see a return for their money. With this in mind, we wrote a five-year plan with the intention of opening eight shops and then selling. We have achieved that and more, and have actually been able to give the investors their money back four times over and keep most of our shares. We opened the second shop in Fulham a year after the first and the third one in Kensington about six months later.

Our ultimate goal now is to have a country-wide chain of Sweaty Betty. Some people pay £10,000 for surveys. Our market research is just a question of going to Starbucks in the area we're thinking of opening up in and evaluating our target market. Once we've expanded nationwide, we'll sell the business and take some time off, but my dream is to go global, New York, Sydney. But that's all down to franchising. I'm on the lookout for the right deal.

I was 28 when I opened the first shop, and I was in a pretty good place to do it from, but you can do it regardless of the situation. There's always a way. So long as you're passionate about what you're doing and you're prepared to really go for it. You've got to live and feel what you want to do. You must be doing it for your soul and then it'll work, even when on paper it looks like it might not.

When the first Sweaty Betty store opened in Notting Hill, my best friend, Jeanine, lived around the corner from it and raved about it non-stop. The minute she described it to me I knew it was a winner as, like Tamara, I had long despaired of the awful gym gear on offer on the high street in large chains that I shan't name! I also knew a few women at the time who had talked and talked about setting up a Sweaty Betty-type shop, but none of them did anything about it. It was a brilliant idea, just waiting for someone to take the initiative and run with it. Tamara was that person.

Effort Is Not the Same as Struggle

There's a saying that once you start doing what you love, you never work another day in your life. There's a lot of truth in that. All the people in this chapter, and indeed throughout this book, love what they do, choose to do things they enjoy doing and are interested in. Eamonn Holmes often works eighteen hours a day. In the early days, Trisha Mason started work at 8 p.m. after putting the kids to bed and worked until 2 a.m. Tamara Hill-Norton thought nothing of working an 84-hour week. Are they workaholics? Well, it depends on the definition. Eamonn, Trisha and Tamara all put tremendous effort into what they do, but there's no struggle, conflict or tension in any of their activities. On the other hand, to work this hard on something you loathed would be a phenomenal struggle and very, very exhausting. The Puritans said, 'Hard work never did anyone any harm.' Well, that depends on how much fun you're having!

Work smart and eliminate as much conflict, compromise and struggle from your life as possible. Don't fight with yourself to fit into a role that just doesn't suit you. Don't try to squeeze yourself into a position that you'll never feel good in. People often come to me and complain about their jobs when actually, the jobs are fine. They're just the wrong person for the job. It's the fit of them and it that's the problem.

What Do You Really, *Really* Want to Do?

Be honest and ask yourself right now how you feel about everything you do in your life. If you didn't have to do any of it, what would you do instead? Jot down all your roles and responsibilities and give them a score between 0 and 10, 10 being 'brilliant' and 0 being 'loathsome'. I appreciate that life involves compromise and a certain amount of obligations, but beyond those, how much struggle is built into your life? How much of what you do is 'loathsome'? Hopefully none or very little, but imagine how you'd feel if the balance in your life was tipped overwhelmingly in favour of 'brilliant'!

Ensure that what you're busy doing is what you really want to be doing. Occasionally, check in with yourself and ask the question, 'Do I really want this?' It's very easy to keep busy doing what you think you should do, what others think you should be doing, or what makes good career or financial sense. But, what do *you* think? Do you really, *really* want to be doing this? Remember, there's no point in being busy just for the sake of it.

Watch What You Do

Time and energy are both precious commodities, to be prized and guarded. Eamonn Holmes watched his father work long, hard hours for no great reward. He learnt that hard work is not an end in itself. That awareness has helped make Eamonn the strong negotiator he is today. We all have to make choices about how we spend our limited time and energy. When the author J. K. Rowling was asked how she had managed to write the first Harry Potter book as a cash-strapped single parent, she said quite seriously that she didn't do any housework for four years. There's a woman who knows her priorities!

Calm Down in Order to Do More

Gandhi used to say that the busier he was, the more he needed to meditate. In other words, while everyone else is running around in circles, you have to be the one who keeps their head, maintaining a strong, calm centre. Don't tolerate drama and chaos, in yourself, once you're over 30. Looking and feeling 'all over the place' dissipates your energy and focus, blurring the path of your goals and the direction of your entire life as well as wasting precious time and possibly costing you expensive mistakes. You might look like you're doing a lot but are you actually achieving the results you want?

A strong, centred person is one who conserves energy by spending it wisely, moving in a clear, straightforward manner. Decisions come from clarity and action from deep consideration.

Cultivate the habit of regular meditation to promote a still centre. It doesn't have to be complicated; just sitting still in a quiet room for fifteen minutes a day will do. If you're new to this, keep pen and paper handy to jot down anything you might want to remember afterwards. Your mind will be busy and it will take time to be able to switch off your internal chatter. Don't have an agenda other than resting your mind and body. Alternatively, t'ai chi or yoga will bring the same state of internal calm and control. It's also a good idea to spend enough time in your own company to know your own mind. The mark of genius is the love of solitude. So declared Leonardo da Vinci, who believed that only in solitude could he truly become himself – or, rather, only then could he fully experience the vision of himself that he kept before him. Only in solitude could he draw on the full power of his mind and imagination working together.

I've seen many ambitious achievers burn out prematurely and never fully regain their original health and vitality. A successful life has to include good health, otherwise your success comes at too high a price. I've also seen people too busy to pull back and have fun, their frenzy of activity draining any joy from their lives. I should know as I used to be one of those people! As a go-getting Capricorn, I had to schedule 'fun' and 'rest' into my diary, otherwise all work and no play made me very dull and tired indeed.

Whatever You Do, Be Happy

Paddi Lund was a conventional dentist in Queensland, Australia. But the pressure and stress of running a practice that most people dread to visit, drove him over the edge. Dentists have one of the highest suicide rates of any profession in the world. Paddi didn't go that far but his breakdown nearly thirty years ago made him rethink his approach to work. He decided that he couldn't keep going unless he and his team began to enjoy their work more and from that point on he would only do things that made him happy. He made happiness his ultimate goal and began to consider what it would take to achieve it in his work. What followed was a period of incredible innovation in all areas.

First off, he decided that he would only work with patients whom he really liked and that all new patients had to be referred by existing patients. There's a sign on the doorbell of his locked front door, 'By Invitation Only!' and he removed his name from the phone book. He sawed up his reception desk and replaced it with a café bar, a large Italian espresso machine and a convection oven where he bakes fresh 'dental buns' for his patients. You don't 'wait' in a waiting room with others. You have your own personal lounge (your name and photograph are on the door) where you enjoy tea and coffee with your care nurse in Royal Doulton china from a silver service! Paddi now only works three days a week but he earns more than three and a half times the average dentist – and he doesn't charge higher fees.

Most importantly, Paddi is happy and his team members, whom he calls his business family, are happy too. That's clear because they don't leave the practice. Three of Paddi's care nurses have been with him for more than fifteen years. Patients rave to all their friends and pay their bills on time, often in advance. This simple approach to life and work is laid out in his book, *Building the Happiness Centred Business*, the same book that England's most successful rugby coach, Sir Clive Woodward, handed out to his 2003 World Cup winning team and urged them to read, saying, 'It's the only business book I've ever read twice.' He credits Paddi Lund with having 'changed his approach to business, rugby and life'.

Money Isn't Everything

In our commerce-driven world, it's sometimes difficult to get in touch with what you'd really like to do, or do more of. Take a break from thinking about the bottom line so that you can focus your thoughts on things you really enjoy doing. Give yourself a week to simply imagine these various scenarios. Sleep on it. Pay attention to how you feel about them. It could be that you decide to set something up that isn't your primary money earner but pays enormous dividends in the satisfaction and joy it gives you. If your dream is to have your own winery, for example, but you don't see how it can make you wealthy – does it have to? Could you be content with it paying its way, producing sensational wine in a beautiful part of the world that you now have a home in? The possibility always exists that the care and attention you lavish on this venture may make it take off in a way you are surprised by. Remember that Paddi Lund made his business more successful in every way, including commercially, once he set out to be happy. At the end of your week's commercial break, choose up to three ventures that you would like to explore. Put some effort into researching these interests with a view to choosing one that you want to invest time and energy into. The criteria should be that it is something you would do in your ideal world, that lifts your spirit even as you think about it and, finally, that you want to have in your life even if it's not your main source of income.

Jojar 'Joe' Dhinsa was nominated Young Asian Businessman of the Year for 2004 at the age of 29. He is reputed to be worth more than £40 million and is chief executive of the private equity firm, Athlone Group. His greatest joy is making money and his aim is to be a billionaire by the time he is 40. He is the youngest of six children, raised by his Punjabi parents who were penniless when they came to Britain from India in the 1960s. His father, Joginder, who died recently from Parkinson's disease, was illiterate. Neither can his mother, Gurmej, read or write. Thirteen years ago, Jojar's sixth-form tutor – none other than Estelle Morris, the future Education Minister who famously resigned because she felt she was 'not up to the job' – told him he would be 'a nobody'.

Jojar Dhinsa

Being one of six children, I grew up in a two-up, two-down in an area of Coventry that was notorious for drugs and prostitution. We coped with it and made do with what we had. My father came to the UK from India in 1958 for a holiday, intending to make some money to send back home. He ended up staying here for the rest of his life. We try and play catch-up as immigrants but tend not to look back. My father and mother had it harder than us because they couldn't speak English. They had every handicap except for being handicapped. Dad learnt a little bit of English as he went along but even now when Mum's watching TV she doesn't understand – she just watches the pictures.

What drove me from such a young age was that I knew money was going to play an important role in my life and I knew I wasn't going to be rich living off my mother and father. I used to look at how hard my father worked in the cotton industry for

Courtaulds and I realised I wanted some reward for hard work. Because he couldn't speak English, read or write, he couldn't do a supervisor/foreman's role so his job was always manual. Someone once said to him: 'No blacks, no immigrants, and no Irish,' but he didn't understand why a white face was so important. He was six foot six and 22 stone with a deep voice. I think people always assumed he was big, bad and ugly, with a ferocious temper. He always got what he wanted in his own way.

What people don't understand about me is how it's all happened so quickly but you have to bear in mind that I've got twenty-three years of working experience behind me. I have been working since I was six. I desperately wanted a pair of trainers and went to the shop with my father and picked out the ones I wanted: they were £21. When we got to the checkout my father said: 'Well, are you going to pay for them?' I left the shop without the trainers but decided then and there that I'd make my own money and get them. I started a paper round the very next day. The other boys were older than me. They had bikes – I walked. I started before school at 5.30 and finished at 8.30. Then I did another round after school. It was safe enough – one of the benefits of living in a poor area is that everyone knows you and it was safer in those days. The money I earned was mine – it was everything. When I was paid for the first time, I put the money on the mantelpiece and just looked at it. A few weeks later I went back to the shop and got the trainers.

I wanted to turn that £3 from my paper rounds into £30. Being nosy by nature, I started to salvage discarded lawnmowers and electrical items from skips and dumps in upmarket areas. My brother's best mate, Mike, who was ten years older than me, helped with the restoration and then we sold them on. It took off from there. I'm a saver. By the time I was 13, I had saved £1,000 – that's when I knew I'd be really wealthy before I was 20. I was so focused. I channelled all my energy into making money. While other kids drank and partied, I worked, and as a

Sikh, I've never touched alcohol. I became more driven when my brother Ajaiv was killed. I was 14 and he was 26. A week before Christmas a drunk driver crashed into the car in which he was a passenger. I was so angry and grief-stricken that I diverted all my rage and sorrow into work.

By then I had spotted an opportunity to import dyes from India and sell to the factories around Coventry. I saw that I could make plenty of money while undercutting existing importers. When I started the business we didn't have any offices or structure. I was still a teenager so Mike and Eddie, my best friends to this day, helped me out. I used to go to the only decent hotel in Coventry, the De Vere, with a tape recorder and record the background noise of the lobby, then go back to my bedroom and press play to pretend it was a busy office environment!

By the time I was 16 we'd built a business and I had made £500,000. Although I was running a business, I never missed a day of school. In fact, I won the attendance prize! And the funny thing is that at the time Estelle Morris called me into her office and told me I'd always be a nobody, I had a thriving business and £500,000 in the bank. I also went on to take three A-levels and qualify as a chartered surveyor.

I still get a thrill from money – whether it's one pound or one million pounds. If you respect money, money will respect you. It's not racist, prejudiced, sexist – it can be your best friend or your worst enemy. I don't sleep a lot – not because I don't want to, I just can't. I have catnaps in the afternoon, otherwise I think I'd be dead by now. I work, eat and sleep when I want to. The two guaranteed events in our lives are birth and death; the bit in the middle is our decision, our stage to perform on and do whatever we choose. The only person stopping you doing that is you. If you say to yourself, I want to achieve X, Y and Z and you put all your energy in, you will achieve – that's what I do every single day. It's hard. But remember, we can survive anything except death.

If you knock on a hundred doors, one will open – but are

you the sort of person to give up at the 97th? Being successful is like boxing – you fall down, you get up. I fall down all the time. When I moved down south I didn't know anyone. I went into recruitment because I knew I'd get to meet lots of people. I made fifty calls a day, that's a thousand a month. My colleagues were amazed. I still work every hour of the day. Even though I have more than enough in the bank, I see every day as the beginning of my life.

Simple things and ideas are the best – all I do is give people what they really want. We are all building sandcastles – when our tide comes in, it takes it all away. You have to be very selfish, single-minded and self-centred to achieve your goals but at the same time, you don't have to be nasty about it. I tell people what I want up front. I'm switched on seven days a week – everything in my life is an opportunity. I want to be an MP and eventually be the first Indian Prime Minister because I'm from the grassroots and straight-talking. And I'll never forget where I came from.

The main thing to register about Joe's story is that so much of life is a numbers game. He who makes more calls, knocks on more doors, puts in the greatest effort, stands the greatest chance of success. Bear in mind his telling comment, too: 'All I do is give people what they really want.' In other words, ensure that there's a need and a market for what you're selling. And in life we're always selling something!

Joe's attitude makes him invincible. Should he lose all his wealth tomorrow, he wouldn't be floored for long. His determination and drive would have him running around, selling something that enough people want, to get back on his feet again. Don't forget, he's been doing deals since he was six or seven, when he foraged in posh people's skips, revamped what he found and sold on. At 29, he has more experience of human psychology, the art of persuasion, and succeeding, than the average 45-year-old.

Five Steps to Do More!

1. Proceed boldly. Many a false step is made by standing still. Action creates its own momentum. Get in the flow by getting busy. Create a feeling of urgency by doing more in less time, and then take the rest of the day off.

2. Act first. Think later. Turn your to-do list upside down. Do the most daunting thing first, without dwelling on it. Don't give it a moment's thought. Just dial the number. Just do it.

3. Tell the truth. What do you really, *really* want to do? If you're going to do more, you might as well do more of what you want, rather than what you don't want.

4. Don't waste time. Focus your efforts to produce the maximum return on your time and energy. Understand what you do best and concentrate on that. Delegate what you don't enjoy or excel at to others. Know your niche.

5. Have fun. Don't become a busy bore. Doing more of what you want should make you happier and more irresistible to be around. If not, step off the treadmill. You need a day off. And, being more dynamic and all-round effective should leave you with more time to play with.

4: *Take* MORE RISKS

There's a saying that the more exciting the life, the more risks there are in it. I know for sure that making do with what we don't really want, or never going for what we really do want, in the name of 'security' or 'safety', may not be a good enough answer for us. I'm not advocating recklessness, of course, but I'm suggesting that being too frightened to take risks is deadly, and one of the key inhibitors of success.

In their book, *Life Lessons: How Our Mortality Can Teach Us about Life and Living*, Elisabeth Kubler-Ross and David Kessler talk about the lessons they learnt through their work with the dying and those who have survived life-threatening illnesses. And the most important lesson we can learn from those that have looked death in the eye? To let go of fear. The authors write: 'So much is possible when fear no longer holds us captive. To transcend fear, we have to practise. If you tackle your secret passions, you will not face regrets of a life half lived. We all have our dreams. But, sadly, we are also filled with reasons why we shouldn't fulfil them. Life is over sooner than we think.'

Having worked with people who have stared death in the face and come back, I know from experience that these people don't mess around once they get their second chance. A young woman I worked with, whom I'll call Jane, survived the 1999 Paddington rail crash in which thirty-one people died and hundreds more were injured. She suffered serious spinal and head injuries, making a return to work impossible for a long period, and will require physiotherapy and monitoring for the rest of her life. In the weeks that followed the crash Jane was gradually able to admit the truth about how she felt about the life she had led. At 34, she had outgrown the man she married ten years earlier and her gruelling daily commute from Berkshire into central London was 'killing her'. For a long time she had felt something had to give, but had then decided that nothing was that bad and those around her led similar lives. Her husband wasn't a bad person either. He enjoyed a quiet life, content with running his small, manageable driving-school business. Her job with a large insurance company was reasonably well paid but she overworked, put too much into it. On the day of the crash, 5 October, she had taken an early train to get into work to prepare for a day of meetings. If she hadn't been so conscientious she would have taken her usual train, thirty minutes later.

Jane never did go back to work, at least not to her old job. In the long days and months of her recovery, she found solace in the beautiful cottage that she had spent so little time in. She discovered peace and stillness in nature, the changing seasons, the trees, woodland and flowers around her. Her strength began to return through working in her garden. This became her new world and eventually she opened the most exquisite flower and plant shop in her local village. She now works with a different kind of busyness, more measured, purposeful, than the frantic whirl of before. And her husband? This was the hardest part. She finally let him go, leaving herself free to live alone for the first time in her life. Surprisingly, he didn't seem to mind that much.

It took a near-fatal, life-changing event to force Jane to give up the security of a job and a relationship she knew were wrong and risk everything for the chance of real success and happiness. But it needn't be that dramatic. I want to embolden you through meeting four brilliant individuals who have taken risks, failed, picked themselves up and used failure to their advantage, emerging with resilience and experience to benefit their next venture. This is particularly evident with Nick Jones and Iqbal Wahhab, whom we'll meet shortly. It's no coincidence that they are both in the restaurant business, one of the riskiest and most failure-prone of markets.

The Value of Failure

I mentioned Tina Brown's success in the previous chapter and how at the height of her powers she was known as the 'best editor in the world' and 'the Queen of New York'. She appeared invincible, unstoppable. With the success of *Vanity Fair* and the *New Yorker* magazines behind her, the publishing world wondered what Tina would do next. In 1999 came the launch of *Talk*, the upmarket celebrity and gossip magazine, of which she had been appointed editor. It was an event attended by the powerbrokers of American society, from showbusiness, to fashion, to politics. Photographs of Tina and her famous friends were beamed across the world. But *Talk* closed after two and a half years. Tina had failed for the first time in her life and it was a very public defeat. Everyone had an opinion on it and many could hardly contain their glee. Dismissing her critics, she said, 'There is nothing more boring than the undefeated. Any great, long career has at least one flame-out in it.' How amazing is that? In New York recently, I watched her on CNBC hosting her own prime-time business talk show, *Topic A*, looking every inch the polished TV anchorwoman. She had made a spectacular comeback but New York's media pundits couldn't agree on whether it was working or not. US television is cut-throat and if Tina doesn't make the ratings, she won't be there for long. She's taking a major risk, and as I write this, I've just heard that Tina has pulled the plug on her show or had it axed, if you believe the gossip. The last *Topic A* was screened on 29 May 2005. Tina's next project in her 'great, long career' is a book about Princess Diana, for which she will be paid a massive $2 million.

One of the greatest myths about successful people is that they have somehow achieved that success without any pain, disappointment or defeat. On the contrary, look beneath the surface of any great achiever's career and you'll find more than one 'flame-out'. You may have to look deeply as they won't be publicising their mistakes, but they're there. Sir Richard Branson, Virgin boss and the UK's most popular and successful entrepreneur, once said of his success, 'I've just failed a lot more than most people,' and on another occasion, 'The best developer of a leader is failure.'

Famous 'Failures'

Take a look at some great achievers who were labelled 'failures' or hopeless at some point in their lives. Use this list as an inspiration and a reminder that failure doesn't have to be disastrous and the prospect of it doesn't have to be terrifying.

Albert Einstein, considered the greatest genius of the twentieth century, was four years old before he could speak.

Babe Ruth, basketball legend and one of the top home-run hitters of all time, struck out 1,300 times.

Beethoven's music teacher once said of him, 'As a composer, he is hopeless.'

F. W. Woolworth, one of the founders of the modern department store, got a job in a dry goods store when he was 21, but his employer would not allow him to wait on customers because he 'didn't have enough sense to close a sale'.

Isaac Newton, the great scientist, did poorly at school and was considered 'unpromising'.

J. K. Rowling is Britain's highest-earning woman with a personal fortune in excess of £200 million. The first Harry Potter book was turned down by eight agents, and when she finally got a deal, she was warned by the publisher, 'You'll never make any money out of children's books, Jo.'

Thomas Edison was told by his teacher that he was too stupid to learn anything and encouraged to think of a career where he might succeed by virtue of his pleasant personality.

Walt Disney was fired by a newspaper editor because he 'lacked imagination and had no good ideas'.

Winston Churchill had to repeat a year of school after he failed the test that would have allowed him to move up a year.

The Meaning of Failure

Failure tests us. It has the power either to crush us or diminish us for ever, or to awaken reserves of courage, resilience, adaptability and perseverance. Failure can define you or be the making of you. Whatever the circumstances, whatever the event, how you experience its impact is entirely your choice. You may canvass opinions and interpretations but, eventually, you will have to decide who you are in the aftermath of failure.

A few years ago I was a guest on a daytime TV chat show. As it happened, this particular episode was especially interesting, being on the theme of 'Breakdowns and Breakthroughs', and many people's stories were both shocking and inspirational. As I was leaving the studio, one middle-aged man asked to speak to me.

Mark's story was no worse than many others I'd heard that day: he had been made bankrupt, losing what had once been a successful hotel business and a comfortable lifestyle with private schools for his two daughters, ponies and stables at his home and plenty of expensive holidays. Now his wife had left him and he was living in a bedsit, depending on state benefits. He was crushed. At 52, he felt washed up and finished. He no longer believed in himself but he was smart enough to see that it was his outlook that was condemning him and robbing him of hope, rather than his actual circumstances. He knew that he had to stop thinking of himself as such a total loser, otherwise he would spend the rest of his life in a damp bedsit. I agreed to help.

My job was to kick-start Mark's reserves of hope, self-belief, enthusiasm and optimism. Then, to devise a plan of action to get him back into the game again. Before that, however, he needed to acquire a new perspective on everything that had happened to him. He needed to stop wallowing in blame and self-loathing, both of which are exhausting and time-consuming, leaving little time or energy for anything else. Getting over things required forgiveness from himself, understanding that he had done what he had thought best at the time. That said, the fact that he had made mistakes and errors of judgement also had to be faced head on. If we don't learn from the mistakes of the past, we repeat them. Within four weeks, Mark was recovering his old spirit, and wiser and smarter than before, free of the weight of guilt that he had been collapsing under. He was ready to join the ranks of the workers once again: he not only wanted his life back but was prepared to fight for it. I left him applying for hotel and retail management jobs and six weeks later, he emailed to say he had landed a job, running a small country hotel, with comfortable accommodation included. He had moved out of the bedsit!

Being able to handle failure is something to get good at. It's an intrinsic part of any lively, ambitious life. There doesn't seem to be any escape or hiding place from it. From what I've seen, the more you try to avoid risk and the possibility of failure, the more difficult life is when it finally catches up with you. The renowned author of the best-selling *Anatomy of the Spirit* and *Why People Don't Heal and How They Can*, Caroline Myss, says, 'The absence of courage causes more suffering than can ever be calculated.' We all have our individual, personalised challenges in life, but failure is universal. It's something we all have in common, so it's best to face the prospect of it now and get entirely comfortable with it. 'Those who overcome themselves are strong,' wrote the ancient sage Lao-tzu. So, it's time to ask yourself some straight questions. Understanding your attitude to failure is crucial if you are going to allow yourself to be inspired by the risk-takers' stories in the following pages and throw off the fear that gets in the way of success.

What Do You Think about Risks and Failure?

Finish off these statements with the first three answers that come to mind.

My biggest fear about taking a risk is . . .

The worst thing about failure is . . .

What I feel about myself when I fail is . . .

What I think others may think of me if I fail is . . .

What I get to avoid through not taking a risk is . . .

Don't Personalise Failure

I want to emphasise that failure is universal. Every single one of us has let ourself or others down. So, with this in mind, ask yourself: is there anything you need to forgive yourself for? Are there any ghosts you need to lay to rest? Is there any failure or past mistake you need to draw a line under? The Americans call it closure. Right now, jot down any past situation that you feel still haunts you to some extent. Then, make a note of the valuable lessons that experience has brought or could bring you. Remember, the Chinese symbol for change represents crisis/opportunity. Every disappointment carries within it the seed of its own transformation. If you don't believe me, think back to a time in your own life when this was true. Remember an incident that initially seemed disastrous, but turned out to be a blessing, that allowed you to go on to something much better. If you still can't recall one, keep thinking and looking.

We've all come across people who, though devastated at the time, credit a redundancy as the greatest blessing in disguise: it acted as a wake-up call to push them into making a long overdue change. Lance Armstrong has just won his seventh Tour de France. He reckons that his recent battle with cancer has actually made him a better athlete due to the fact that he endured so much pain while having treatment that his pain threshold during a gruelling race gives him an edge over his competitors. That really does prove the adage that if something doesn't kill you, it can make you stronger. I reckon that if I asked Hollywood heart-throb Colin Farrell to pinpoint the defining moment of his career, he'd point to a day back in 1993 when he failed an audition in Dublin for the boy band, Boyzone. Manager Louis Walsh told him he simply couldn't sing. With hindsight, what a blessing that failure turned out to be! After it, Colin decided to concentrate on acting, headed off to Hollywood, where his first role was in Joel Schumacher's *Tigerland*, launching an incredible career that currently pays him $7 million per movie, probably more by the time you're reading this. Boyzone, as we know, is no more.

Seeking scapegoats is counterproductive, as accepting responsibility is vital to encourage the reflection needed to resolve a problem. I've heard it said that a person may make mistakes, but isn't a failure until they start blaming someone else. Significant failure such as the end of a marriage or business bankruptcy demands a hard look at yourself. How did your behaviour and decisions contribute? Was arrogance or procrastination a contributing cause? Apply this line of inquiry to both personal and professional issues. If failure, real or imagined, feels like a hard thing to resolve on your own, don't hesitate to have a deep conversation about it with a trusted friend, colleague or life coach.

It's easier to take risks when you're cushioned by the support of a comfortable family background providing a financial safety net. But what if that's missing and your family actually advise you against taking a risk and to stay on a safer, more predictable route? This was precisely the case with my next case study, Alexander Amosu. When I mentioned to my 14-year-old son, Jamie, that I was meeting Alexander, he begged me to let him come with me, insisting that he could learn so much more from Alexander than he would at school. As I listened to Alexander talk, I wished that Jamie could have been there to hear his story. Alexander is a hero to teenagers because he is a mobile-phone ringtone millionaire. He is Britain's most successful seller of mobile-phone tones. Labelled 'the Lord of the Ringtones' by the media, Alexander's turnover was £1.2 million in his first year and in 2002 he was named Young Entrepreneur of the Year at the Institute of Directors' Black Enterprise Awards.

Born in London, to Nigerian parents, Alexander spent the first couple of years of his life in the capital, moving back to Nigeria when he was two. At 12, he returned to London to live with his grandmother and younger brother in Wood Green, north London. There was so little room in their council house that Alexander had to sleep on the sofa in the sitting room. It was in 2000, when he was 24, that he accidentally stumbled on his lucrative career, though his rags-to-riches story begins much earlier.

Alexander Amosu

When I came back to England from Nigeria it was a real culture shock because I couldn't fit into any of the groups at school. I was different and I couldn't understand that. I wanted to be in with the cool kids who had the Nike trainers but actually I didn't even have enough money for school dinners. I had really geeky and ugly clothes. So at the age of 13, I started doing a paper round, getting up 6.30 a.m., and delivering newspapers every day for £10 a week.

In fact, at first I considered stealing money to buy things to help me fit in with the other kids, but I didn't really believe that that was my strength; I was too scared! But it was easy for me to wake up early, deliver the papers, save my £10 for five weeks and then eventually buy my Nike trainers. I put them on, showed them to my grandmother, who was proud of what I'd achieved, went to school and got a fantastic response from my peer group.

I was always, always looking for ways to make money. When I was 16 and resitting my GCSEs I put on a football tournament. I got the school's pitch for free, charged each player £5 to enter and bought a medallion for £3.50 and a trophy for £10 for the winner. I made a £750 profit. I put on six more tournaments in other sports and branched out to put on parties and inter-college events, like a Valentine's Ball.

One day during my first year at North London University, where I was studying computer-aided engineering, my aunt who was heavily pregnant asked me to clean her house. So I cleaned the house, and when she gave me £20 as I left, I thought about the number of other people who must be in a similar position. I knew I needed to earn money to live on so I decided to take a chance on setting up my own company. I called it the Care Cleaning Agency and the first thing I did was design an advertising flyer on my home PC. I printed off 5,000 leaflets and personally went round putting them through letterboxes in my local area.

A week later, I had my first interview with a potential customer. It was like my first adult interaction with the world and I wasn't prepared for it. As soon as I got into her house, I could tell that I wouldn't get the job because I was a kid. I didn't look professional and I didn't have a licence or insurance. So I left that meeting thinking that I'd learnt something. When I got another call, I bought a suit, photocopied my passport and birth certificate and mentioned my mum as a referee. I offered to clean the woman's house free of charge for a week and sure enough she employed me. My belief is that with every no, there's always a yes. If someone says no to you, that's a problem and you have to find a solution. You've got to find the reason for that 'no' and counterbalance it with something else.

By the time I sold the company, three years after I worked for that first client, I had twenty-one cleaning contracts and was employing staff via the JobCentre, paying them £5 an hour and keeping £5 for myself. The business grew through being listed in the Yellow Pages and advertising in a local newspaper until we were taking about £1,500 a month. It was the most difficult job that I've ever done because it's a very complex and intimate thing when you enter people's homes. There were a lot of problems if the house wasn't cleaned properly or if something got damaged. I found it hard to manage but I learnt from every mistake that I made and eventually sold on the company for just under £19,000.

There have been moments in my life when I've had to really believe in myself and be passionate about what I was doing to justify a big risk. When I was in my final year of university, I came up with the idea for the R&B Ringtones website. I only had about four or five months left of my engineering course but I told my dad that I was going to leave because I believed so strongly in this idea. He just couldn't understand why I'd wasted three years to go and play with mobile phones. Coming from a Nigerian background, there is a pressure to have a significant degree and become a doctor or lawyer. I respect my parents and it was very sad to go against their wishes but I really believed that that was the best thing for me at the time.

My big idea came when I sent my brother a ringtone I had made. It was 'Big Pimpin' by Jay-Z. At the time, 2000, most people only had the ringtone that came with their phone, so when my brother's phone went off at college all his friends immediately wanted it. I invited them all over and charged them £1 for the ringtone. By the end of the day I had made £7. I thought, 'What would happen if I made a catalogue of ringtones and advertised it?' My brain went into work mode. I did some research and found only one company in the UK and several in Germany providing ringtones. I decided to specialise in R&B music and, within six weeks, came up with another six ringtones. I installed an extra phone line, with a premium-rate number charging £1.50 a minute, in the council house I was living in with my parents and I advertised the number on the back of 20,000 flyers that I had had printed for my next party.

On the first day R&B Ringtones made £97. I gave up university. Four months later I moved the business out of my parents' house into two offices in Islington and had twenty-one people working for me, selling 1,000 ringtones. We were making the songs all day long as they were coming out. It took off like a rocket. Within a year we had a £1 million turnover.

I believe in education but I don't think it's the only tool in life. I think we should also teach our children how to make money off their own backs so that they're not reliant on getting a job to survive. I've been doing a lot of talks in schools and communities along these lines and when I have more time, I will eventually open a school where children can learn how to make money work for them and not the other way round.

I never fully believed that I would make millions but I always tried to make enough money to be able to invest it in whatever I saw around me that had potential. Lots of other things I've tried to do have failed. I spent £1,000 buying old tin cans and lamps to sell on at car-boot sales but I only sold half my stock and ended up making a loss. I like failing, though, because I really believe it makes me stronger and I see it as a learning curve.

I've never blamed my failures on the colour of my skin and I believe people who say that are holding themselves back. I've learnt a lot from being in business and now I only seem to deal with white people. In this environment you have to be able to adapt to people and not think that everyone you're dealing with is racist because it just won't work. I make sure that I get what I want regardless of what people think of me.

Three years after starting up R&B Ringtones I sold 80 per cent of the business to give me the cash to set up mobsvideo.com, which provides 30 second clips for mobile phones, and soon I want to be able to expand it to entire programmes and films. I know I'll succeed again. I tell everyone, Motivation plus determination equals success. If you have that, no one can stop you. If I can do it, you can do it.

The crucial thing I wish my son Jamie had been able to learn from a meeting with Alexander was how simple, straightforward and fearless his attitude and approach to life are. This brilliant combination has led to amazing success. He makes things happen by just having a go and giving it his best shot: not everything has worked out, but that's fine, and something to be learnt from. When he set up the cleaning company, he just printed off the flyers and walked the streets near his home, putting them through letterboxes. There was no weighing up the pros and cons or working out a business plan. If it worked, it worked. When his first potential customer declined, he figured out why, wore a suit to meet the next one, and got the job.

Alexander emphasised to me his total amazement at how simple it is to take a great idea and run with it and how many great ideas there are lying around, waiting for someone to take a risk with them. He admits he knew nothing about the technical side of producing ringtones, but that didn't stop him from making it happen, and he was astonished that no one had already done it. Nor did he invent the technology that will make mobsvideo.com a success, but so what? 'I know nothing about building a house,' he said. 'But I guarantee that if I wanted to build one, then I'd do the research and I'd know what there was to know. I find out what needs to be done.'

Talking to Alexander made me think of something Philip Beresford, the compiler of the *Sunday Times* Rich List, once said: 'We can all talk up a good idea in the pub, but 99.9 per cent of the population never does anything about it. A money-maker will get up the next morning and, even with a massive hangover, have the confidence to turn that idea into a money-spinner.'

I don't know about the hangover as Alexander prefers squash to champagne, but he's definitely among the one per cent who'd be up the next morning making calls to check out that good idea.

The Fear of Failure

On 24 February 2003, during the deadest month of the year for the French catering world, a day when only ten people ate lunch in his Michelin three-star restaurant, the Côte d'Or in Saulieu, rural Burgundy, Bernard Loiseau, one of the most successful chefs of his generation, put a gun to his head, killing himself instantly. Why? In 1991 he had been given the ultimate accolade for a chef – his third Michelin star. But that which blessed the young chef also cursed him. Bernard dreaded failure as much as he had craved success. The need to hold on to those three stars tormented him. His nightmare was to lose his fame, his business and – above all – his stars.

The tragedy of Bernard was not that he was about to lose his three stars (he wasn't) but that he *thought* he was. In fact, his reputation was not in danger, but so dependent was he on that external validation of his standing that it drove him to pull the trigger. Albert Einstein said that 'Unthinking respect for authority is the greatest enemy of truth.' It was Bernard Loiseau's unthinking respect for the authority of the Michelin judges and restaurant critics that proved his greatest enemy. It was no accident that he shot himself on the eve of the 2003 Michelin Guide's appearance.

Who Says It's a Failure?

If failure is a universal experience, it is also a hugely subjective one. Of course we all have responsibilities, but we also owe it to ourselves to remember that at the end of the day it's our life. In fact, a healthy disregard for the good opinion of others is vital for your enduring success *and* psychological wellbeing. So says a unique survey of 300 British millionaires carried out in 2003 for the BBC2 television series, *Mind of a Millionaire*. Undertaken by the agency Tulip Financial Research, the survey found that half of those owning their own business said that it didn't bother them if others around them disapproved of what they did. The richer the person, the more likely they were to see themselves as self-reliant, enthusiastic and dedicated to success.

This entrepreneurial trait runs through all of the great achievers in this book, regardless of whether their venture was a business or a charity. It's blatantly true of the individuals you'll meet in this chapter.

When creating any new business or undertaking any new activity, you're likely to be greeted with scepticism and disbelief, so you have to develop a skin that is thick enough to allow you to make up your own mind, independent of the good opinion of others. This lack of need for validation from others is an intrinsic part of the make-up of all the millionaires interviewed for the Tulip survey and every inspiring person I've ever met or read about. It's a crucial factor in deciding whether to follow a hunch and take a risk. Remember that Alexander Amosu's father begged him not to abandon his university studies, four months before his final exams? He felt that Alexander could play with ringtones in his spare time. 'But I knew that I had to make my own choices and that if I did make a mistake, then I'd learn from it,' Andrew told him. 'I have to have control over my life: sometimes I may be right, sometimes I may make mistakes, but it has to be me who makes the decisions for me.'

Nick Jones's first two London restaurants were total flops, and he ended up owing the bank more than £1 million. Ignoring his critics, he carried on and opened the hugely successful Café Bohème. In 1995, when he founded the trendy private members' club, Soho House, his friends warned him not to. When he bought Babington House, a large, run-down country mansion in Somerset, in order to turn it into a stylish hotel, he got the same advice: Don't do it. The Electric Cinema in Notting Hill, west London, had been running at a loss for years. Jones took it over anyway: 'They said "it didn't work before why should it work now?" I've heard it all,' says Nick. 'But I'm best when my back is against the wall.'

Nick was running his first restaurant, Over The Top, on

London's Fulham Broadway in 1988. It was intended to be the first of a chain of burger/steak bars where customers chose their own combinations of toppings. I used to pass Over The Top every weekend, as I had friends in the area. But although we did eat out together, we never liked the look of Over The Top: it felt cold and uninviting and it was always empty. It was a huge space, right in the middle of Fulham Broadway, an area packed with busy bars and restaurants full of City yuppies and estate agents who prided themselves on being able to afford to eat out most evenings. But not at Over The Top. Another branch, in Soho, was doing no better. A million pounds in the red, the bank gave Nick one more chance. Today, Nick's Soho House business is valued at £33 million in the UK. Soho House New York opened in 2003 and was in profit after only six months. Its showbiz credentials were assured when its rooftop pool was featured in an episode of *Sex and the City*.

Nick Jones

I was very lucky that I experienced failure because it really did teach me how not to run a restaurant. Failure is a good thing because if you've got the character to be able to take all the positives out, it means you're better equipped for success. You just need to make sure that you don't repeat the same mistakes. The next time round I did everything the opposite way.

There were several flaws with the Over The Top concept but the biggest was that all the toppings were disgusting. I remember sitting in one of the restaurants in the middle of the lunchtime rush and the place was empty. I couldn't blame the recession because people still eat in recessions – it was empty because the whole place was unappealing. The décor was revolting, the service was shabby.

After two years Over The Top closed in Fulham and I turned the Soho one into Café Bohème, where I just reversed everything

I'd done before. Rather than a lunch restaurant with a fussy concept, I went for late-night licensing and created a brasserie serving fresh, simple food from eight in the morning until three in the morning. Then the office space above the café became available and the landlord, Paul Raymond, offered it to me at a really good deal. My shareholders begged me not to go for it as we'd just come through five years of financial nightmare. There was no shopfront, only a narrow doorway, with stairs leading up to the other floors, so I realised it would only work as a private members' club. Given that it had once been a house and it was in Soho, I called it Soho House. Why complicate matters?

The only real business research I'd ever done in my life was on Over The Top, which at the time everyone thought was a great idea. I went back to the era of following my gut and that's the way I've stayed. I cobbled together a committee of people I'd met at Café Bohème who worked in television – agents, actors and writers – and threw a 'Hard Hats at the House' party. It was literally 'hard hats' because Soho House was still a building site at the time. All the committee members asked twenty friends and somehow it worked. People had a great time, paid £250 each for founder membership and we opened six months later (1995) with 500 members. I've just held a party for our tenth anniversary for those original members. Today, the annual subscription is £500. We have 4,000 members and 2,000 on the waiting list.

One of my secrets is that the market I attract is just like me, and for that reason I can really relate to it. If I like something, then I think there's a load of people out there who want the same sort of things. My hobbies are eating, drinking and napping and that's what my business is all about. I love having a good time, going to restaurants and staying in hotels.

In 1998 I opened Babington House, a sort of country-home-from-home for our members. I knew there was a demand for something rural with a London ethos. We took the rule book, tore it up and started letting people do what they wanted – if they felt like breakfast at five in the afternoon, we'd cook it for 'em. Babington has been full from the day it opened.

Opening Soho House in New York was a huge gamble. It was a much grander venture than London and New York is the most competitive restaurant market in the world. Hotels and restaurants open and close there continuously. I knew I was setting my sights high. Ian Schrager in New York *magazine accused me of 'trying to import the class system' and 'bringing over the obnoxious London media culture which encourages an awful in-and-outness'. That did get to me. I mean, I wasn't taking on New York. Schrager didn't need to lose any sleep over what I was doing.*

I chose the Meatpacking district because it appealed to me and had the same combination of edginess and character that Soho has in London. I found an empty electronics warehouse and decided not to rip it up completely, but to keep the wooden beams and original brickwork, which is unusual for a New York hotel. I saw it as a playground for New Yorkers, so you'll find pool tables, pinball machines, a spa, cinema, late licence. The style and furniture is a scattering of vintage and modern. We opened in April 2003 and now have 2,500 members and are ahead of budget.

Success is something you've got to work so hard at: the moment you take your foot off the pedal is the moment success deserts you. If you're running any company, you've got to be seen to be putting in a lot of effort and working very hard. There are very few examples of success without hard work, unless you are extremely lucky, and even luck comes through hard work. You've got to listen to your customers, and the great thing about a club is that you have a committee comprised of your customers. If you don't react to what they say, more fool you.

What I try and drum into the people I work with is if you make a mistake, just put your hand up and admit it. Then everyone can forget it and move on. If you believe in something, really go for it straight away and don't wait two or three years. I probably set up in business too early because I was impatient and didn't have the experience and that's why it all went wrong. But then, where else do you learn to run a business? You don't learn it in someone else's company, you have to get out there and do it yourself.

I may open another Soho House in LA, Miami, or perhaps the Hamptons. Or maybe, Spain or the South of France. There are all sorts of possibilities but I'm not after global domination. I just don't want myself or my customers to get bored. When I'm older and sitting in my rocking chair, I'd like to think at least I've always taken risks and given things a go, even if not all of my projects have worked out. That's how you can judge your life – by looking at what worked and what didn't. I'd hate to sit there and think, 'If only.'

The fact that Soho House is the inspiration of the same man who ran Over The Top is incredible. One thing it proves is there's nothing like failure, especially spectacular failure, to teach you valuable lessons.

Mind you, even when you're as good as Nick Jones is now, things can still go wrong. As a founding member of the London club, in April 2003 I flew to New York to be one of the first to stay in the new club. My excitement was not in the least diminished by the panicky long-distance calls in the days beforehand to explain that the kitchen wasn't quite ready. Not a problem for me. As long as I could stay there, I could eat anywhere else. As my yellow cab turned the corner of Ninth Avenue to head up to Soho House New York, I could see a frenzy of activity outside. Cabs and limos lined the street, a small crowd was gathered outside, and the foyer was similarly busy. The paparazzi perhaps? Already? I spotted the familiar faces of London staff and members. How exciting! Truly home-from-home.

An eager-to-please chap ran to greet me and explain that 1) I shouldn't panic and 2) there was a 'situation' (he was a New Yorker!) that he needed to explain to me. The New York fire department had made a visit that very morning, the opening day, to inform the management that under no circumstances would any guest be staying there that night or any other night for some weeks to come.

I wasn't happy. And I wasn't the only one, as grumpy Londoners poured out and into cabs bound for alternative hotels. For weeks I'd pictured myself sitting in the upstairs lounge, sipping a Cosmopolitan, people-watching on to the very same streets that the *Sex and the City* girls used to hang out in. I was in heaven just thinking about it. And now, it wasn't going to happen. Like I say, I wasn't happy.

This could have been a total PR disaster, but Nick handled it with such grace and generosity that it wasn't. It was just one of those 'situations' that come up in life. We were ferried in complimentary limos to nearby boutique hotels to find a letter of apology from Nick, a bottle of chilled champagne and an invitation to stay for free – as soon as the club actually opened. So, even when you're Nick Jones, the worst can still happen! And I'm sure Nick learnt valuable lessons from that experience – at least where the NYFD are concerned!

The point I'm making here is that failure comes in many forms, but that there are very few situations that cannot be improved by acknowledging the problem, taking action to deal with it promptly and apologising to those affected. If you can recognise that failure doesn't have to mean disaster, you're much more likely to take some valuable lessons away with you. This positive attitude to risk-taking is embodied in our next case study.

In 2001 Iqbal Wahhab opened the Cinnamon Club in Westminster, London, with the radical agenda to serve Indian cuisine in a Michelin star-type restaurant. There wasn't, and still isn't, anything else like it in the world. It was a brave move. Iqbal had no experience of the notoriously competitive restaurant trade. He had worked as a journalist and run his own PR business up until then. Building work on the site took a year longer than planned and went £750,000 over budget. Iqbal remortgaged his flat twice to raise money and the bank tried to put him into receivership three weeks before the Cinnamon Club was due to open. Today, it has an annual turnover of roughly £5 million and in October 2005 Iqbal launched a new restaurant, Roast, dedicated to British cooking and seasonal produce. Future plans include a New York-style restaurant in Trafalgar Square, with an Indian nightclub in the basement, and a similar waterside version of this in Canary Wharf.

Iqbal Wahhab

I was brought up in a slightly unorthodox manner. I am the product of my father's experiment in free will. Both my parents were academics. My mother was the principal of a college in Bangladesh (we moved to London when I was nearly one) and imposed a strict regime on my older brother and sister. But my father, a philosopher professor who specialised in the question of free will versus determination, said I should be allowed my freedom without discipline. When I was born he said, 'We won't tell him right from wrong. He can work it out for himself.' Now, I wasn't told this until I was about 25 years old and it really explained a lot. It explained why I could do whatever I wanted and why anything and everything was permitted. It must have started when I was about two years old. I was perched on the edge of the sofa and my mother was concerned that I was going to hurt myself. Dad simply said to leave me: 'He'll realise and stop himself from falling.' Of course I didn't and promptly fell off, was admitted to hospital and to this day the left side of my body doesn't quite work when I walk, but I did survive! So, crazy things like that happened. But it also allowed me to do things that, ordinarily, people wouldn't do or be allowed to do. I was never informed that this was going on. I just thought that, as the youngest, I could get away with anything. I don't remember it being anything other than normal.

I first began to realise that things were different when I was 11 and just starting secondary school. In 1975–6, the National Front was very strong in Battersea, south-west London. Hanging around the school gates, two NF kids used regularly to beat up the brown-skinned kids from my school. I was curious what all this was about, so on my first day I went up to these NF kids and started talking to them, chatting and joking. They were taken aback and I became quite friendly with them. I didn't talk like brown-skinned people were meant to talk. I made them laugh. Later that day they showed me some dirty magazines which they'd stolen from the local newsagent. I bought the porn magazines off them for 10p each and sold them at school for 30p. They were still Nazis but it got me out of trouble and I made money out of them. I made so much money that I could afford to buy a black suit costing £100 from Selfridges as my school uniform. My Asian classmates didn't like me at all – they thought I was just out for myself. Most importantly, it stopped me getting beaten up.

I failed all my O-levels, just like all the kids I was hanging around with. My parents went quiet on me until I had worked out what it was I had to do about it. I returned to school, immersed myself in my studies and I actually quite enjoyed it. I retook my O- and A-levels and got into the London School of Economics to study politics. I became so interested in the subject that in the year before going to college, in the early 1980s, I read every political book I could get my hands on. I wrote a 35-page pamphlet on these books, which nobody wanted to publish, so I decided to publish it myself. I got a job as a porter in a West End block of flats where a lot of wealthy Arabs were living. They were impressed when I told them why I was there. Within a short amount of time, by doing extra personal jobs for them and charging for my services, I had earned the £2,000 I needed to publish my book.

I milk every opportunity for what it is worth. I extract the maximum out of every situation. I was 20 when I published my book. I went to the LSE bookshop, said I'd written a book and persuaded them to put it in the window. So at my first lecture, my name was already familiar and I was known as a published author! I joined the Communist Society because they were looking for a chairman. I nominated myself and somehow I got elected. I wanted the chairmanship because it would give me a platform to go wherever I wanted to go. Then I became editor of the student paper, which was a big thing. I was also on the student executive and had a whale of a time. I set up the Overseas Students Society with 700 members, charging £10 when membership to other societies at the time was 50p! Being head of the Fresher Fair, I made sure that the OSS stall was the first you saw when you entered the hall!

During the 1990s I set up a PR company, East West Communications, representing all the main Indian restaurants. Then I took on a number of European restaurants and one of our flagship restaurants, Pied-à-Terre, was awarded a Michelin star. The experience there was so different from what Indian restaurants were offering that I criticised the standard of British curry houses in an article I wrote in 1998 and all hell broke loose. It was in the papers, on TV. I was banned from restaurants. I received death threats. One group called and said they were coming down from Nottingham and knew where I lived. It was simply that I could see that there was an extra attention to detail that a Michelin star-type restaurant had that Indian restaurants didn't. And that's when I got the idea to do it myself, to create a restaurant just like the one I'd been talking about, to adapt Indian cuisine to contemporary restaurant ways.

I live for the moment and have always been caught up in the passion of an idea. When I first saw the building that is now the Cinnamon Club – a huge (12,000 sq. ft) former Westminster library – I fell in love with it. I used to drive there at weekends and sit in my car outside. All the restaurant developers like Conran and the national brewery chains were after it. As I had no track record, without big money behind me, the property agent refused even to put my name on the list. I knew I had to get past him and go straight to the chairman of the firm selling the building. I phoned him at 8.30 a.m. before his secretary was there to screen calls and asked for just thirty minutes of his time. I admit that I bluffed that I had £1 million and was ready to exchange contracts. I didn't have a bean, right up until Christmas Eve, when I shook hands on the deal. I needed £1.7 million and quickly made calls to City contacts and gathered eighteen shareholders on board, investing from £10,000 to £250,000 each, from their Christmas bonuses.

Being brought up the way I was, I had no one to be answerable to. There was never a notion of letting my parents down. That kind of conversation never happened. I wasn't criticised, punished or pushed to succeed by them, so I could never be a disappointment to them. Consequently, I don't have any regrets. A lot of people put pressure on me to quit the restaurant business before the Cinnamon Club had even opened because it was way over budget. At the time, the BBC were filming me for their Trouble at the Top *programme. My bank manager said he was going to call in the administrators. So I told him to tell that to the camera at 9 a.m. the next day and he backed down. I was shaking when I put the phone down as this was never in the film schedule. It was pure bluff on my part. Even my landlord said he couldn't bear to see me get into trouble because he liked me, and advised me to sell the lease to some contacts of his. He was so decent about it that I agreed to talk to a couple of guys for his sake, not mine. One of the industry's big hotshots was overheard saying: 'My God, how a journalist (me!) thought he could do something with this place I'll never know.'*

That guy made me absolutely determined not to sell up. That one extra piece of motivation was all I needed to open the place and we did so on 4 April 2001. There are a number of people in the restaurant business who can't stand me and resent my higher profile in the media. There are people out there to this day who are doing me down. They don't like the fact that their predictions that I'd never get the Cinnamon Club off the ground have proved wrong. But because they were never active supporters of mine in the first place, what they say about me behind my back doesn't really bother me.

If the restaurant hadn't been a success, I'd have regrouped, bounced back and done something else. I don't entertain failure as a person so if it had gone belly-up, I would have told people it was because of gaps in my knowledge and resolved to learn how I'd do it better next time. I don't think I'm a show-off, I just don't analyse everything to death.

I don't think it's ever easy to take a risk because if it was easy, it wouldn't be a risk. My Indian restaurant magazine was a flop after three issues: it cost about £200,000 of investors' money and around £20K of my own. I thought that because two million adults visit an Indian restaurant every week, there must be room for a consumer magazine, so I set up Indian Food and Drink *in 1998. That was misjudged. Just because people have eaten Indian, it doesn't mean that they want to read about it. I made the mistake of buying into my own hype. I learnt the reasons why it failed and didn't take it personally. It was a really worthy experiment. It had failed but I was going forward. What is seemingly obvious now wasn't necessarily so at the time.*

One very important factor in my story is that as well as my family, I have friends who don't get caught up in my so-called success. They cut me down when I'm talking too much about myself. Another useful thing is having your own little mantra that motivates you. And remember, I haven't cracked any kind of code. I've struggled for five years to get to where I am today.

I had heard a lot about Iqbal before we met. Interestingly, the journalist who had edited his ill-fated magazine spoke only of what an energetic and inspiring chap he was and how people had actually worked without payment to get his new restaurant up and running. So, I was intrigued to find out for myself what Iqbal was like. I arrived to have lunch with him on a freezing January day, traditionally a bleak month for restaurants. But not here. The place was three-quarters full and it was like no other Indian restaurant I'd ever been to. There was no tinkling music or flocked wallpaper, no images of the Raj and not a poppadom in sight. The food was sublime.

What immediately struck me about Iqbal was how easy-going and relaxed he was. I could already imagine that he would be good in a crisis, unflappable and entirely pragmatic. I saw this at first hand when, just as we had ordered our food, a waiter came over to explain that there had been a call to say there was a leak in his flat. I immediately offered to rearrange our lunch so he could leave and sort it out. Without a hint of panic or pretence, he insisted it was no great problem, merely a dodgy dishwasher, nothing that couldn't wait an hour or so. I suppose this was nothing compared to what he'd handled at other times in his life, but what I also saw was someone whose sense of himself, his identity, was so intact that it would never *occur* to him to think of himself as a flop, a fool, a loser, if a project didn't work out. A failed venture was simply something that would require a thorough investigation to understand what had happened in order to avoid the same situation happening again. I felt this had to have a lot to do with his unusual upbringing, where he was cherished and allowed to do pretty much what he wanted, encouraged to take risks and handle the consequences. He grew up with a huge amount of implicit trust and faith from his parents that he would come good in the end.

Perhaps the fact that Iqbal was the only baby to survive a malaria outbreak in the maternity ward where he was born in Rajshahi, Bangladesh, encouraged his parents to see him as special? I realised that I was meeting someone who was untouched by his past failures and not in the least daunted by the fear of failure in the future.

Of the London Cinnamon Club venture, Iqbal says, 'There isn't a single person I can think of who hasn't told me to ditch this project along the way – friends, family, the management team, even the odd shareholder. But I never lost faith in it.' What he really never lost faith in was himself. Unlike the Michelin-starred chef, Bernard Loiseau, he did not have 'unthinking respect' for those around him, but was driven by his own authority and conviction about his project to make it more than just a dream. Even if it hadn't happened, it wouldn't have been the end of the world.

And he didn't mention that leak in his flat once during lunch!

Rethink Failure

Just imagine what it would be like to be as freed-up around risk and failure as Iqbal Wahhab. What would you contemplate? What's your secret passion? What would you really do if you were as fearless as him? Maybe you are already, but I have to say that it's rare to meet people with this much personal freedom. Right now, jot down the answer to this question: If I knew I couldn't fail, what would I do? With the mindset of an Iqbal, you could conquer the world, if you so wished. Once you've conquered yourself, anything is possible.

Remember, it's not failure that is the real problem: it's your attitude to it and how you deal with it. Often this is handed to us as we're growing up, by parents and teachers. You might have been lucky and been encouraged not to fear failure, but even if you weren't, it's never too late to adopt a new attitude that is more useful to you.

My father loved a good risk, so when faced with a patch of black ice on the road, instead of slowing down, he'd speed up on the basis that if it was dangerous we should race through it as quickly as possible. Well, it didn't kill us and it was exciting! We had a shared disrespect for authority, which has been useful to me throughout my life. When I was taking O-levels, if I had no afternoon exams, he would drive up to the back of my school to 'rescue' me for the rest of the day. I'd slip out of a basement window and jump into his van, crouching on the floor until we were out of sight. Then we'd have lunch in a café and I'd go back to work with him in the gas showroom that he ran. His irreverence not only made me laugh, it also helped me to understand that few things in life, even exams, were really about failure, in any black-and-white sense. And it also encouraged in me a healthy wariness for authority and officialdom, then and later!

Think Learning Curve

One of the core assumptions of successful achievers is that 'there is no failure, only feedback'. Others talk of failure as a 'learning curve'. Why not take the negative charge out of the word 'failure' by replacing it with one of these phrases? This may help you to avoid labelling *yourself* a failure, thereby preventing you from assessing a situation clearly and taking decisive action. That is a really crucial point. Whatever you do, never, ever label yourself a failure. And don't keep company with anyone who does, or thinks in this way. It will rub off. Martina Cole never told anyone about her dream to be a successful author. Observing her 'scribbling', her friends would say, 'Working-class people like us don't write books.' So she kept her dreams to herself and focused on what she wanted to achieve, and her crime novels are now best-sellers throughout the world.

Martina grew up in Essex in a large Irish Catholic family, the youngest of five children. Her mother, a psychiatric nurse, was from Dublin, and her father a merchant seaman from Cork. Martina attended a convent school, which she hated and left at 15. The one subject she enjoyed was English. By the age of 19, Martina was a single mother living in a carpetless council flat in Tilbury with her newborn son Christopher. She had no money for a television or socialising, so, after she had put her son to bed, she would write to keep herself entertained.

Married in her early twenties, Martina juggled writing in her spare time with running a home and working, but it wasn't until she was 30 that she decided to devote herself seriously to writing a full-length novel. She gave up her job as a secretary, bought an electric typewriter and told her husband she would 'give it a year'. Many years earlier she had started working on the manuscript of *Dangerous Lady* and it took her eighteen months to complete – the rest is history.

Martina continues to live in Essex with her eight-year-old daughter, Freddie, and is close to her son, Christopher, now 27, and her grandson, also eight. She has written 11 hugely successful novels, the latest of which, *The Take*, was published in October 2005 and went straight to the top of the bestseller lists.

Martina Cole

I trust my instincts. By the time I was 31, I had written numerous books and about one hundred scripts but had never sought publication. One day, I decided to send the script for Dangerous Lady *to the BBC sitcom department. It was unsolicited and I had taken valuable time off work to update this piece that I had written ten years previously. Martin Booth, a BBC script editor at the time, invited me in for a chat. The trouble was, I couldn't remember which one I'd sent in – I'd written so many. I remember the exact words he said to me: 'You have an upfront, confrontational humour, reminiscent of Rosanne.' I thought, Christ! I still didn't know which one he was talking about. I ended up writing new scripts for the BBC, which were always too shocking to be screened.*

I found Darley, my agent, in the telephone book. I just had a good feeling about the name. He asked me to send him my manuscript, as he was intrigued although he didn't really think it could work. I sent it off on the Friday and on the Monday evening I got a phone call that changed my life. I'll never forget the words: 'Martina Cole – you are going to be a star.' He said he had waited all his life to have a book like this to sell at auction. I trusted him implicitly from the moment I met him. He was the first person I'd met who was interested in me as a person, not a unit, a mother, wife or sister. So, we had lots of lunches with publishers. Headline made me a £150K pre-emptive bid and the auction was called off. At that time, it was the highest advance ever paid to an unknown author. More important to me than the money was the thought: someone really wants to read this. Once published, I still didn't think anyone would bother to buy my book. It went into the best-seller lists at number four.

Until that point, Miss Jones, my English teacher, was the only person who had believed in my writing. She used to get so angry with me because I was always playing truant from school, smoking and not doing any work. My mum and dad were members of the library but never knew it. I joined on their behalf and got out six adult books a week. I used to read these books all day long in the park: Ernest Hemingway, Harper Lee and John Steinbeck and books that my dad brought back from his travels. I still remember him bringing home The Godfather. *I started it at about midnight and the next morning my mum came in from work at eight to wake me up for school and I was on the last chapter. I was inspired by all the books I read and began scribbling stories in exercise books.*

I have always been a free spirit and if I hadn't lived my life the way I have, I'd have nothing to write about. Even as a small child, I never went with the flow. I got expelled from my convent and yet, any job I've ever done, I've done really well. Years ago I was holding down three jobs at once, waitressing in pubs and clubs. I remember the harshness of work. I used to drop Christopher (his father died when he was a baby) off at school in my nightdress if I couldn't be bothered to get dressed because I'd been up all night working. I'd take him to school and then go back to bed. But I kept writing. I wrote the draft of my first novel, Dangerous Lady, *during this time, but I put it away in a cupboard and didn't show it to anyone.*

Ten years later I was working in a nursing agency and I was offered the chance to buy the business. I knew that if I took it on, I would make a go of it, but it would take up every drop of my energy and time. I'd probably have to give up on my secret dream of becoming a writer, so I decided to give myself a year off and see if I could get something published. All I ever wanted was my name on a book in the library. Funnily enough, now my books are the most requested from prison libraries – and the most stolen from shops!

For some reason I have always taken on subjects that are in the public eye but never at the time when I write about them! There will always be an underclass and I write about it. Where we lived, you had to step over the heroin addicts to get in the front door. I used to talk to them, reason with them. But I've always tried to be non-judgemental. Life is a series of kicks in the teeth and you just have to get up and dust yourself down. I have a working knowledge of what I am writing about.

My novel Broken *is about child sex offenders and some people feel they can't read it. My argument is that if I can educate people while they are having a good read, then why not? Someone who initially read the manuscript said it was too shocking for publication but I didn't care. I was willing to take the risk. I try to put opinions that I loathe into my books. I see every side of an argument, always have. Sometimes there's more to life and people than meets the eye.*

The biggest risk I've ever taken was getting married. Since then, I've done all the things I never thought would be possible – like seeing my work adapted on Broadway. I like risks, they lead to great things. You only get one life. No one can afford to be too complacent. Some people spend their whole lives trying to make the right decisions, stay safe, be secure, but there will always be shocks which is why you must take chances.

So few of us achieve the things we really want, but I did. It's taken perseverance. If you don't work for something, you don't achieve anything. I used to care, deep down, what people thought about my books but I don't apologise for anything now. I still write for me, not for an audience. If I'd tried to get my work published when I first wrote it, it would have been rejected because the market wasn't ready for it. So actually it was a good thing to wait until I was 31. If Darley had said no to me, I would have thought: One down, one hundred to go.

I'm a patron of Women's Aid and when I talk to women there, I always say: Don't put your happiness in someone else's hands. Keep your happiness in your own hands. Still to this day, women rely on men for their happiness. I never did. I'm very independent and perfectly happy as I am.

When I had my son everybody wrote me off. But I still felt I could do something with my life. I never gave up inside although I never told a soul because they would have laughed at me. People used to say to me: 'You're still scribbling, Martine! You want to grow up.' When I got published the same people said: 'Oh, we always knew you'd make it!'

Within ten days of posting off *Dangerous Lady* to a London agent who was no more than a name in the phone book, Martina was on her way to a new life. What a sensational story! If it wasn't actually true, you'd never believe it! But, bear in mind, she had been 'scribbling' since she was 13. She used to 'see' in her mind a book with her name on the cover and dream of a life where she was a successful author. And she kept that dream alive for all those years. Her luck only kicked in after she took the risk of giving up the security of a regular salary to do everything she could to make the dream happen. Sure, she had talent. But, how many other people let their talents go to waste, without risking putting them to the test?

I 'discovered' Martina Cole during the Christmas holiday of 2004. In a reflective mood, I decided I'd been watching far too much television and should read more. The fact that the tube in the television blew on Boxing Day (strange but true), two weeks after the guarantee had expired, helped cement my new resolution! I headed off to my local bookshop the next day and bought the number-one title on the best-seller list: Martina Cole's *The Graft*. I spent the next seven days, and most of the nights, wrapped up in her underworld. I got through *The Graft*, *The Know* and *Faceless*, transported to a parallel world of crime, drug dealers, prostitutes, pimps, paedophiles and bent coppers! It was a long time since I'd come across such a brilliant storyteller.

A month later we met at Martina's favourite restaurant, PJs in Covent Garden, where I'd heard she had her own table, with a brass plaque with her name on it. Martina arrived, looking every inch the glamorous, blonde, best-selling author that you see on her book covers. What you might not notice is the steely toughness behind the look, which I've only seen in older people, or maybe just in people who've lived a lot. We sat down at her table at 4 p.m. and for the next five hours she held me spellbound with stories of her early life. She talked of her instinct and how it had sustained and guided her throughout her life, and then, abruptly, squeezed my arm and asked me a strange question. She asked me what my middle name was. Taken aback,

I had to think. I only have one middle name and it's – Martina! Now that's instinct so good, it's weird.

In life you must be willing to take chances in order to achieve your goals. The most common excuse I hear from people who don't pursue their big idea is that 'there's no guarantee'. How true, and this is something to really grasp and go beyond. None of the individuals in this chapter had any guarantees before they made the leap from a great idea to acting on it. Martina gave up a paid job to give herself a chance to finish her book and become a writer; Iqbal held true to his vision while friends and investors advised him to sell; Nick opened a members' club in Soho *and* a country house hotel against all advice, followed by an English club in New York; and Alexander stood his ground against his own father when he walked away from completing his degree to follow his big idea. What all these individuals demonstrated was a faith in their own instinct – and a willingness to follow that instinct. Even when they got things wrong, like Nick and Iqbal did, they picked themselves up and moved on swiftly, armed with valuable lessons and information. Winston Churchill defined a successful person as 'Somebody who goes from one failure to another without any loss of enthusiasm.' Ensure that's you!

Five Steps to Take More Risks

1. Don't let others pull you down. The world is full of people who will tell you why your schemes won't work. Sometimes you have to rely on your own inner resources and be selective about who you listen to. Think carefully and then select your advisers. Constructive criticism, not automatic dismissal, is what you're after.

2. Use a mantra. Propel yourself forward with the right message. *I can do it, I will find a way, I'm good enough to do this*, will all put a spring in your step. These are your holy words, with the power to sharpen your focus and create your results. Soon enough, they'll kick in and start working for you.

3. Develop your instinct. Save time and money by trusting your gut instinct more. You may not need market research if you trust what you're seeing and feeling. Ask yourself what you 'feel' about people rather than what you 'think' about them. Do you trust them or not? What's your sixth sense telling you?

4. Take more everyday risks. A risk a day keeps boredom at bay. Enjoy trying something different without any guarantee of a successful outcome. Even trying out a new restaurant gives you a fresh experience and stops you from getting stale and set in your ways. Doing different things keeps you risk-friendly, even on a small scale. It all adds up to a bigger outlook.

5. What's your secret passion? Think bolder thoughts. Why on earth should the fact that something is seemingly impossible prevent you from trying, with all your might?

5: *Inspire* OTHERS

There's only so much you can achieve on your own. Whether you want to start a revolution, rid your country of a colonial power, create an incredible business, get elected to parliament or simply find a way to live life on your own terms, you need the co-operation of other people to do it. You need to be able to inspire others.

For many years my father was a travelling salesman for Hoover, selling washing machines and vacuum cleaners door-to-door. He was a magnificent salesman, the best the company in Northern Ireland had ever had. When he wasn't selling, he was reading books like *How to Win Friends and Influence People* and would hand down his nuggets of wisdom to me. Thirty years down the line, one in particular is imprinted on my mind: 'The best way to get someone to do something is to get them to *want* to do it.' Obvious though it sounds, this simple truth, like much common sense, isn't that common. But it is at the heart of true power and influence.

This ability to inspire has to be one of the most compelling characteristics of great achievers and it's been a feature of success throughout human history. All great leaders know the value of it. Jesus of Nazareth, Alexander the Great, Joan of Arc, Oliver Cromwell, Fidel Castro, Rosa Parks, Emily Pankhurst, Winston Churchill, Martin Luther King, Nelson

Mandela and Margaret Thatcher all understood the importance of inspiring others to achieve victory.

Great Inspirers

Without this ability, how else could one man have rallied his country to overthrow a powerful imperial power? Mahatma Gandhi didn't need to resort to violence and neither he nor his supporters had great wealth on their side. What they had was one man's passion and his capacity to communicate it to vast numbers of people. Shortly after Gandhi, in another continent, another man would use this same incredible ability to rally huge numbers of his countrymen to follow his dream of making Germany a world power. Hitler was a master at inflaming a crowd's emotions so they would do anything to fulfil that dream. This genius for inspiring others can be used for good or evil. Its power lies in the ability to persuade others to want what you want, as much as you want it. How you use this talent is entirely down to you. I'm going to assume and hope that it's for your good and the good of all.

Great inspirers aren't necessarily great orators, making stirring speeches to vast crowds. Often, they ignite a spark in others that spreads way beyond their initial action. Rosa Parks was one such inspirer. Rosa was a black seamstress living in Montgomery, Alabama, in the 1950s. Civil rights were not yet on the agenda in America's Deep South. City buses were segregated, with only white people allowed to sit at the front. One day, in December 1955, Rosa was asked by the driver to move to the back of the bus. On this particular day, Rosa refused, was arrested, and her arrest sparked a boycott of the segregated bus system in Montgomery. She refused to be treated as a second-class citizen because she was an African American. Soon, others followed. Living in the same town, and inspired by her example, was a young preacher called Martin Luther King. Rosa's action brought the world's media to Montgomery and led to ten years of marches, speeches and an entire campaign of equal-rights activism, before the segregation laws were finally ended.

Once you touch people's hearts so that they want the same as you, as much as you, you could have a revolution on your hands. Once a great idea takes hold and grips people's imagination, there's no telling where it might lead. As I write this, six young Catholic women from Belfast are preparing to meet President Bush in Washington. After that, they'll meet Senator Hillary Clinton, Senator Edward Kennedy and others, as honoured guests of the White House 2005 St Patrick's Day festivities. The world's media will record their every move and utterance, as they have done for the past six weeks. The women are the sisters and fiancée of Robert McCartney, who was stabbed to death in a Belfast bar at the end of January. Their insistence that the culprits, who the family know to be members of the IRA, be brought to justice has inspired other Catholic families who have had family members murdered or maimed by the IRA to speak out in spite of their fear of intimidation. The story of the McCartney family's defiance in such a climate has touched hearts everywhere. They emphasise that their campaign is not just about their own personal crusade for justice for their brother: but for a new climate of justice in Northern Ireland, so that other families will never have to suffer what they have.

Great inspirers are really quite rare. I haven't seen too many. What I see more often is an individual with passion and enthusiasm for something, which drives them into action, but without the ability to persuade others to feel the same way. Stirring that desire and longing in others is something else altogether. The commonest mistake I see in passionate people, and I've made it myself, is assuming that your passion is naturally contagious. Not necessarily, and you could end up feeling both frustrated and exhausted by continually revving up your own passion and not being able to inspire it in others.

When I spot a great inspirer, I listen and learn. I've brought together four such individuals here, who personify this ability powerfully. Victory is different for each of them, but their stories are hugely inspiring in themselves. Implement this rule in your own life and you'll achieve far more than you ever could without it.

One of the smartest people you'll ever come across is Carmel McConnell. Carmel's life revolves around inspiring others. It has given her a lucrative career and enabled her to create the incredible charity, the Magic Breakfast, that provides healthy breakfasts for over 100,000 inner-city schoolchildren. Carmel is a global corporate business consultant, advising organisations, including leading consumer brands and investment banks, on change management. She encourages them to get ethical, take moral stands – while increasing their profits. She is the best-selling author of *Change Activist*, *Soultrader*, and *Make Money, Be Happy*.

Carmel McConnell

We must be the change we want to see in the world. It's about service and I believe that very strongly. My mum died when I was nine and my dad raised my sister and me in an environment that was about optimism. He was an historian when he lived in Northern Ireland but in England he had to work in a foundry. He had an astonishing memory and a real awareness of how fascinating people are. I was raised with a strong sense of all life's possibilities and I miss him every day. My living a life that inspires me – that is the challenge. Making the best of all that I've been given – that's the joy. I am, of course, a complete optimist but remind myself daily of the natural cycles of life and its fragility. Everything goes up and down. Some days I have what I call my 'Fat Failure Days'. I now know they are part of life and accept them. When you're having one, just acknowledge that you can't do everything and be very kind to yourself.

To motivate others, you need sheer clarity of purpose, empathy, and the ability to build a coalition. There are so many different approaches to building a team. We all need the humility to build with people who are greater than us. To make a big thing happen, I assemble the best people possible around me who have superior skills. Even if they run me ragged! I believe I'm the best person to guide the Magic Breakfast at the moment but in the future, maybe not. Should there be a better way to do it, then fine. You have to have continuing belief in the cause and the problem being solved through whatever means. Inspirational leadership needs to be challenged by the coalition. I am absolutely irrelevant – I have made sure there are no images of me on any publicity material because it's about solving the problem, not about me.

How can your motivational charge ignite someone else? You have to invoke the 'What's in it for you?' question. My rule is: I will succeed in my goals by first of all helping other people achieve their goals. Inspirational leadership is simply brokerage. I am a social broker between those who want to do something but are not sure what and those who would appreciate some help but don't know where from. I love this wonderful bringing together of gorgeous people who have a desire to make a difference. That brokerage is the core of social activism. Through the day-to-day chaos of trying to make our personal economy work, we lose hope that we can define our own great purpose and I think this is one of the great issues of our time.

Once I have become clear on what I want to do, I look at who in the world might be interested in solving this problem with me. I call it my stakeholder map – I write it all down. I genuinely put myself in their shoes and ask the question, 'What would be in it for them?'

In 1985 I joined the Greenham Common Peace Camp and became part of a small group united in purpose and strong enough to stay calm even when placed in prison. I dropped out of university to join the Peace Camp and found my own kind of change activism through the passionate commitment of those around me. The knowledge that action can make a difference has stayed with me. In 1989, I needed to earn money because I had family responsibilities after my father died. So I went to work at BT as a secretary, aiming to carry on campaigning at weekends. Instead I learnt to use my activism there! By applying the same activist ideals, I got promoted every year, attained my MBA and ended up leading a very large IT team. These principles are the same as those deployed by Gandhi, Mandela and even Anita Roddick of The Body Shop. Firstly, clarity of objective is vital because it can reach the parts of us that are motivated by a noble cause. I constantly have to deal with people who have ten number-one priorities – their agendas are so complex. And usually too overwhelming!

I left BT with the theory that if people understood what their company was trying to do and felt respected, then the business would grow. So I started my own company, Holistic Management, in 1995, working on leadership development and growth in major corporates. It was a great adventure, very successful, and I travelled all over the world. Then I came across the staggering statistic that one in four schoolchildren in the UK are malnourished and hungry and I could not believe it. That was in 2001.

I saw that Britain ranks 23 out of 29 in the international league of children with malnutrition. I felt compelled to do something for these kids who had all their lives ahead of them. I just wanted to make sure they were well fed and able to learn.

For the first eight months I would get up every Saturday morning and go and buy food for five schools in Hackney, which is one of the UK's poorest boroughs. I wanted to do more so I dedicated three days a week to research and discovered these protein-enriched wheat bagels. You need carbohydrate to make your brain work in the morning. This wonderful woman, Kris Engle from The Great American Bagel Factory, let me have the bagels for 14p each when they retail at 80p and I spent six months delivering them to schools. During the first year I provided about 3,000 breakfasts, the second year 25,000 and last year 70,000. We think there are about three-quarters of a million children going to school hungry in the UK. So that's the target and I know we can do it.

We are now reaching some of the poorest schools in London – that represents 150,000 bagels a year! I do some speaking events based on change activism and charge a professional rate for that but had to remortgage my house two years ago to keep me going because I don't earn a penny from the Magic Breakfast. We have an administrator and a publicist who are wonderful professionals working for around a quarter of their market value because they want to be involved in a project that makes a difference. Our trustees are professionally very diverse and challenging. I also started a company called Magic Outcomes, which is now the main source of the Magic Breakfast's money. It's a social enterprise and won a Social Entrepreneur of the Future award last year. Basically it is a not-for-profit training firm, taking people from large organisations through a range of development programmes, placing them in our schools and offering them a chance to make a difference. They take assemblies, meet the head teacher, and work with the kids: Pearson, BT and Unilever are signed up and doing programmes with us. People in large organisations say, 'We want to build trust and we want to live our values.' I say, 'Instead of going off to a hotel and doing the theory, come to a school where you can do it in practice. We've put together this fantastic programme, the first community-based MBA.'

A nine-month programme costs £7,000. It costs us £2,700 to run and every penny of profit goes back into the Magic Breakfast to expand and pay for more food for the children. I'm really pleased with how well it's going. One of my passions is helping people to find their purpose – be they children or adults.

Another scheme called 'Adopt a School' gives companies a chance to make a difference. A donation of £1,000 per annum will pay for a breakfast club for a year. If companies want to do more than that, they can, and we'll give them ways to develop their skills in return.

There is so much goodwill out there. People want to be generous. The Magic Breakfast office is in a prestigious central London location and the market value is at least £80,000 per year. My publisher, Pearson, have given it to me because they believe in the Magic Breakfast. I was running this project out of a room in my house but it was getting really tricky to host forums with teachers and nutritionists in such a cramped environment, so I put the word out. I was expecting a room out of town somewhere but through various people understanding and supporting what I was trying to do, Sir David Bell suggested these rooms in Covent Garden. We just pay the rates on it so we are very, very lucky. This space attracts volunteers and improves our credibility. My publisher Rachael Anderson – an inspiration if ever there was one – published a book called Get Ahead and Give a Damn *that perfectly highlights the ideals of change activism. The profits have now paid for a career counsellor for the homeless. All I ever do is give people the opportunity to be generous with themselves, to live their purpose and their dreams. I am constantly inspired by the people I meet.*

I first heard of Carmel McConnell in 2002 when a client invited me to the opening of her photographic exhibition, explaining that a fascinating woman called Carmel would be there whom she described as 'a high-flyer, who also feeds breakfast to inner-city schoolkids'. Although we'd both been at Greenham Common at the same time, our paths hadn't crossed there: and while I had been arrested many times, Carmel had the added kudos of having served a two-week prison sentence! Nearly four years later, I knew she was a natural for this chapter on inspiration.

We later met up at the Magic Breakfast office and I admit that the first thing that impressed me was – the office. The Magic Breakfast occupies the entire floor of a beautiful white Georgian house in the middle of Covent Garden, with vast rooms and ceiling-to-floor windows overlooking the Piazza. I'd sat in many charity offices before, but none that looked like this. I knew Carmel had inspired someone so much that they had given her this space. I then listened enthralled for two hours as she explained, quite simply, how to inspire others. As I sat there, I understood the mistakes I had made years earlier in my political campaigning days and saw how I could have been more effective, less intimidating, and a darn sight happier as well! For your benefit and mine, I've distilled her strategy into five specific steps. Follow it to the letter and you'll see the benefits. I know I will. There are many more things to learn about inspiration from the other case studies in this chapter but I want you to focus on this strategy before we move on to them. This is the bedrock.

Inspire Others – The Strategy

1. State your purpose clearly. Be precise and succinct about what you want to achieve, in a few simple lines, the first being the most important. For example, 'The Magic Breakfast provides nutritious breakfast food to primary schools in most need. Free of charge. No child should miss out on their future success because they lack fuel for learning at the start of the school day. We are an optimistic, pro-active charity that believes this is a food poverty problem that can be solved – here and now.' End of message. Clearly, concisely and boldly stated.

2. Empathise with others. Put yourself in their shoes. Why would they want to co-operate with you and your cause? What would make them want to join your team? Think, 'What's in it for *them*?' Use Carmel's mantra: 'I will succeed in my objectives by helping others achieve theirs.'

3. Avoid egos, especially your own. You need to build a team of smart people, smarter than you in some areas, to get the job done. There can be no room for bullies or insecure egos. Put your team together and encourage people to do what they're great at. Let everyone star and take a lead role. Build success on co-operation, not rivalry:

4. Encourage ownership. Don't make victory personal to you. Make it personal to everyone. Ensure that it's not *your* campaign but *the* campaign. People will give their all to a great vision or purpose, but not to one that is your *personal* mission, for your greater glory. Take yourself out of the picture and put the purpose up there for all to see.

5. Uplift people. Bring out the best in others by seeing their value and appreciating it. Expect the best. Anticipate generosity. Give them your trust. People grow and shine with praise and encouragement and shrink with neglect and criticism. Support each person to stretch to their full height by sprinkling encouragement and appreciation over them at every opportunity.

If I'm really honest, Carmel didn't actually add step number 5. I did. But, trust me, it's a part of her strategy. It's so much a part of who she is, that I suspect she doesn't even notice it's there or that she's doing it. From my first call and in all my subsequent dealings with her I've felt genuinely praised and uplifted by her. And it's not fake or flattery. That's easy to dismiss. I came away from our meeting buzzing with ideas as to how I could support her and help generate income for her, so she can keep on devoting her time to the Magic Breakfast. That's why you'll find Carmel McConnell and the Magic Breakfast promoted on my website today. She tapped into a well of generosity that I felt bubbling through me long after I left her.

Interestingly, I've heard something similar about Sir Richard Branson, the flamboyant founder of the Virgin organisation. People close to him call it his magic dust when describing the effect he has on staff as he quietly encourages them to rise to a new challenge. After a few minutes tête-à-tête, individuals appear brighter and more enthusiastic, fired up and brimming with renewed confidence and vigour, feeling far more able to get on with the job.

I wanted to understand how a commercial venture runs on inspiration. I can see that having a great cause like feeding hungry children can affect people, but how do you inspire people from a commercial environment in your own profit-making business? I was keen to find a sensationally successful business leader who uses inspiration to fuel their success. I trawled the *Sunday Times* Rich List and found the perfect person.

Emma Harrison, a 42-year-old mother of four, is worth a reputed £80 million. She set up Action for Employment (A4e) in 1993, which has a turnover of £60 million and 1,500 staff in more than a hundred offices around the UK. For the past two years A4e has been among the country's fastest-growing companies. The company is a major player in the government's public–private partnership and the New Deal programme, joining with public sector organisations to train people to find work. This year, more than 50,000 unemployed people will pass through A4e's doors. It helps a 'client' into a job every ten minutes. On top of that, Emma is national chair of the NSPCC FULL STOP Campaign, for which A4e aims to raise £1 million by next year.

Emma Harrison

It doesn't matter how inspiring you think you are – without communication skills you actually can't deliver. At 14, I was fund-raising for a blind child at my school. I got the whole school to come to my auctions and raised enough money to send him to America. I became a pupil governor at the age of 15 by getting everyone to vote for me. I've always had the ability to encourage people. I guess it's something to do with my parenting. Although they didn't have a lot of money, I had a very creative mother and a father who encouraged us to use our imagination, thinking and friendships to make the most of the world that we lived in.

I went to the local comprehensive and messed up my A-levels – my mum was ill and I was looking after her. I joined the Health and Safety Executive as a trainee engineer and enrolled at a local technical college to take a course in engineering. I managed to get into Bradford University to study mechanical engineering. My dad ran a small industrial training business, had remarried and wanted to go and live in Germany. He offered the business to me on a fifty-fifty basis, saying he'd give me eighteen months' training to get the hang of it. Eighteen days later, he left, saying, 'You've got the hang of it, I'm off' and he legged it to Germany. At 23 I found myself in charge of a firm with a turnover of £100,000 a year, employing five or six staff and training a hundred people.

I thought, What the hell do I do now? It was a question of survival like it had been all my life. All I knew was that there were three things a business must do: marketing, marketing and marketing. I just went out and found anybody in the government and the Manpower Services Commission who wanted to spend money and asked what they wanted to spend it on. No one ever thought of selling like that. Within the year, turnover was up to £1 million. But success brought its own problems. Suddenly, a family that wasn't wealthy had become wealthy. After a few years, my father returned and rekindled his interest in the business. I decided to walk away, just like that. I was 29 and I left with four colleagues. I had the promise of one contract, for £3 million, from what is now the Department for Work and Pensions, to train people. It was the most difficult thing I've done in my life, very, very upsetting. Because it was my dad and I loved him.

Even though I run a profit-orientated business, I never set out to make money in my new venture, Action for Employment. I have always wanted to help people. I do believe that's why I've been so successful. I set out to retrain unemployed engineers from the steel industry at a time when the industry was in collapse. It came as a massive shock when I was told I'd turned over £1 million. People don't join us to make money for a big corporate organisation. The work I do with my teams across the country is about improving people's lives.

What we choose to do with the money is the interesting part. At A4e we reinvest it and do more the year after. This is a concept that people struggle with but when they get to know the business, they suddenly realise that it works, and this ethos has proved to be incredibly successful. We don't have any budgets at the front line. We spend whatever it takes to improve a person's life. We negotiate the contracts with the government – the more effective we are, the more we get paid. We also work with small businesses to improve them so they can employ more people. The company does a massive variety of things – from numeracy and literacy for asylum-seekers to helping child-care businesses and schools improve themselves. We only work in the social agenda but that area is massive. We do things where we can have a positive effect.

The buzz in my business comes from improving people's lives. I can get to secure a job for someone who has been unemployed for fifteen years. Now that's bloody brilliant. At A4e we offer whatever works for that individual. Before a member of my staff says 'no' to a reasonable request that somebody makes of us, they have to ring me first. And I'm still waiting for that call! This is so fundamental to my business – they have to say 'yes', regardless of the cost. Let me give you an example. A young woman from Exeter came to us who had been on benefits for years. It turned out she was a champion rock climber but wouldn't take any work that would detract from her dream job. She said it just wasn't possible. She wanted to swing off skyscrapers in London doing rope access work, which is an incredibly skilled job but the course cost £10,000. I am so proud of my staff because they agreed to fund it. She now earns a fortune doing what she wants to do. The next guy who walks in might only need a haircut and a revamped CV to find employment. When you get a 50-year-old-guy a job, he cries. He says his wife will love him again! I want to help people move their life on. The training is just a product.

I spend most of my time thinking about how to encourage, inspire and elevate other people. I employ like-minded people who are good at what they do. I am driven by a purpose and I have fun and think hard. I have so many ideas about what we can do next. I sit down and dream about them with my top team but we never go down the acquisition route. I nurture the project, then as soon as it has some life, I pull it out to give it some sunshine and let it develop in its own right. I surround myself with brilliant people and that original gem of an idea doesn't end up stifled under a vast organisation. I'm chairman of the company and I have a group chief executive, who beneath him has a range of chief executives with their own teams for each project we're running – about eight at the moment – and the ideas we're developing.

If you can't trust people, how can you let things grow and develop? The greatest thrill for me is seeing something develop that I've had very little input in. I get so excited about that. My company has just become the largest workforce support for the unemployed in Wales and I haven't yet been to visit any of the twelve new centres we've opened because I trust my people from day one. There's no option but to trust people. They don't have to earn my trust. Not to trust them is destructive. Of course I've been let down but I always say, 'I can't legislate for the lunatic.' One in a thousand people will let you down but the minute you use that to colour your judgement about the people you are working with, you've gone wrong.

My not being involved in each and every project doesn't mean I have disappeared. It simply means I step up and leave the space beneath me to allow other people to grow, develop, explore, enjoy – all those fabulous things. I always try to think how would I like to be treated – the empathy stuff – and make it right for them.

I certainly don't believe you have to pay more to earn more loyalty. People have to be properly paid but they also need to be rewarded with thanks. Nobody at our senior level has ever left because of money issues. Buying people's loyalty is horrendous. The word loyalty is out-of-date in business anyway. I don't want loyalty. I want passion, fun, excitement and belonging. I want my staff to to take pleasure in what we are achieving and creating together. I believe in supporting people to get the best out of themselves for themselves as well as others.

I don't offer share options because they increase greed and self-interest rather than bolster the common goals. I own 100 per cent of the shares in A4e and as far as I'm concerned this bears no relation to the decisions we make and how we run the business. I introduced an idea called stakeholder shares instead, which are totally made up but they reflect what I think is important, i.e., people training and developing themselves and then using that within the business – it's been ever so successful. The more they learn, which is the most valuable thing they can do in the business, the more shares they are awarded. And every year they stay, they get more. The cleaner gets them too – they get the same as a top person. Everyone is at the same level and we pay out dividends every quarter. So we pay out the profits dependent on who has been doing training and who has been with us year after year.

I didn't need to go to business school to learn that the greatest management skill is to be able to simplify, clarify and to focus. People seem to overcomplicate what they do by talking instead of taking action. We're not consultants, we deliver.

I now work only one day a week on A4e but have other businesses too, chairing around six companies. I try to take Monday and Friday off to spend time with my children. Once a year we meet up for what we call One Vision, where everybody talks about their input. It's not about making more money – it's actually now about taking our vision internationally.

Are you thinking what I'm thinking? That Emma Harrison's drive and motivation are remarkably similar to Carmel McConnell's. One runs an incredibly profitable business and the other runs a not-for-profit charity. Both are driven – and drive others – with a vision of a better world. This is fascinating. When A4e hold their yearly conference, they don't discuss the bottom line, budgets and turnover. Their One Vision get-together is all about just that, their vision for improving people's lives – internationally. Now, that's something to get excited about, and clearly, Emma's staff do.

Make no mistake though. Emma Harrison is no soft and woolly do-gooder. When talking to her, I was left in no doubt that this was a dynamic and decisive operator. There is nothing sentimental about her approach to individuals who either sabotage her trust or who aren't doing the job that needs doing. To her, the issue is simple: 'You need a great person doing a great job.' As a coach I have worked with numerous CEOs, managing directors and vice-presidents over the years and I assure you, many of them struggle to attain this degree of dynamic clarity. Facing up to an issue and dealing with it courageously and with kindness is not easy for many people, however senior they may be. And this type of procrastination and inertia can often run right through a company, with the wrong people doing the wrong job – for years.

Emma showed this courage and clarity when she made what was probably the most difficult decision of her life. Walking away from working with her father and their joint company was something she knew had to be done if she was to fulfil her potential to improve people's lives. How many people struggle for years, sometimes for ever, in a family business, desperately frustrated or suppressed, never brave enough to do what they know they should? As a result of Emma's courage on that day, more than 500,000 people have been helped to move their life on by A4e. Remember. Ruthless on the issue, kind on the people.

One Vision

Carmel and Emma demonstrate the importance of having a vision. It emboldens you as a person and makes you stand out. It fuels your life with a sense of importance and purpose. Your entire persona will reflect this drive and vitality. Consequently, you're a more highly charged person, one whom others will be naturally drawn to. You've got charisma. I absolutely believe that it is impossible to inspire others without a vision. The first step to mastering the ability to inspire is to have a clear understanding of your own vision.

Companies often call this vision their mission statements and these came in for a lot of criticism in the 1980s, often seen as nothing more than marketing waffle. A credible mission statement or vision has to be brought to life and translated into meaningful everyday life for everyone. As Carmel advised: Keep your purpose simply stated. Both her and Emma's can be summed up in just four words: *to improve people's lives.*

Winston Churchill said, 'Never doubt that a small group of thoughtful, committed people can change the world. Indeed it is the only thing that ever has.' This was one of the sayings that underpinned the winning mindset of the 2003 England rugby team. Another was that of business guru Sir John Harvey-Jones: 'To create success, EVERYONE'S noses must be pointing in the same direction.' When the English team beat Australia on 22 November 2003 to win the rugby World Cup, it was the first win for England in a major sporting event since the 1966 football World Cup. To ensure that everyone's noses were pointing towards victory, the inspired team coach, Clive Woodward, introduced regular team effectiveness workshops from the moment he arrived in 1997. Sir Clive said, 'If we want England to win, everyone has to see the bigger picture and how they fit in. We have to get them all involved . . . What I want is to bring everyone who has anything to do with the England squad into a room and share the vision of what we're trying to achieve, to get everyone thinking and working in the same direction.'

Reinventing English rugby, 'rebuilding the England squad from the ground up with a new way of thinking', would have the added bonus of 'inspiring the nation with our sporting success' in a way that hadn't happened since 1966, Sir Clive explained in his brilliant autobiography, *Winning!* You can see how the team would have felt stirred to give their all to such a noble cause. This wasn't just about winning a rugby match. It was about doing something great for their country. No wonder the words of Winston Churchill were invoked! Interestingly, the team went on to rename their meeting room the 'War Room'. Later on, they would work with the Royal Marines and learn: *It's not about skills. It's about attitude and the effect on the team. One wrong team player can sap all the energy from the group.*

Over a period of nine months, Sir Clive put together a book for the team encapsulating their mission statement, *This Is England*, which immediately became the cornerstone of the elite culture he was trying to instil in English rugby. The very first page contained an introduction that he hoped would be imprinted on everyone's mind. Here is an extract from it:

> **The Business of Inspiration**
> We are in the business of inspiration. Our job is not only to inspire one another but also all those that we work with, and those who watch us and support us. Our goal is to inspire the whole country.
>
> We are in the business of inspiration – there are no excuses any more. Remember we work in a no 'if only' culture.
>
> We are here to inspire our country – let's do it.
> Clive Woodward
> October 1998

What's Your Vision?

The interesting thing about a vision is that it can be a very simple statement, yet still be immensely powerful. It acts as a guiding principle, a declared standard that you live by and up to. Right now, look at your life and consider what really matters to you. Whatever you do, however you spend your work or leisure time, ask yourself: What's really important to me about this? Don't worry about sounding pious. It's unavoidable. You'll get used to it! Keep it simple. We're looking for a short phrase, a few words, that sum up the importance that you attach to what you do. Why do you do what you do, apart from the money? From now on, think vision with everything, so that you automatically aspire upwards with even seemingly mundane activities. And do take note of the fact that this needs to be a statement, not just a thought. Don't let your vision be vague. Make it concrete – write it down.

Communicate Your Vision

Inspiring others with your vision so they sign up to it is vital – it's the very aim of this chapter and the essence of Rule 5. Your own passion, however intensely felt, is just not enough to ignite the same fervour in others. Ensure that you step out of your passion long enough to see how others will win by joining you. Use the following simple questions to get you into the habit, until it's automatic. Adapt the headings to suit your particular situations.

Plan or Project:

How will the customer win?

How will investors win?

How will team members/members of staff win?

How will I win?

Remember that you fulfil your objectives by first helping others to achieve theirs. Get into the habit of thinking, 'What's in it for *them*?' If in doubt, go right ahead and ask them, 'What's in this for *you*?'

Trust People

How can a mother of four run a company with 1,500 staff as

well as chairing three other companies *and* a committee of a major charity? Here is Emma Harrison's secret: 'Everything I set up has a "without me" philosophy, so that ultimately, it has to be able to run on its own. I believe in instigating, encouraging and elevating and I always recruit people who can show empathy. I don't believe in big egos.' Once she has employed someone, trusting them is automatic. She gives them her trust from day one, because she chooses to. Once her trust is broken, it's broken, but it doesn't stop her from trusting others in exactly the same manner. Showing faith in others is one of the most affirming and morale-boosting things you can do for people. It's a mark of your respect and, in such a climate, people do relax and stretch themselves.

Both Emma and Carmel are two of life's optimists and I guess they wouldn't have it any other way.

Optimism and generosity also characterise my next great inspirer. For over ten years the lawyer Peter McDonnell has funded his campaign to take on the tobacco industry in the courts and on 29 March 2004 the Republic of Ireland became the first country in the world to introduce a nationwide ban on smoking in pubs, restaurants and workplaces. Labelled 'The health initiative of the century', the success of the ban has inspired other countries to follow suit.

Peter made legal history in 1997 as the first Irish solicitor to issue proceedings against the tobacco industry on behalf of people who have suffered a variety of illnesses which their doctors attribute directly to their smoking habits. Peter is claiming that the tobacco companies knowingly and willingly sold a product which caused a variety of illnesses including cancer. He has been approached by thousands of individuals and currently represents over two hundred clients suffering from smoking-related illnesses. He is widely regarded as the leading European lawyer in this area.

Peter McDonnell

You have to keep yourself inspired before you can inspire anybody else. Ten years ago when I was researching the tobacco case, what became blindingly obvious to me was that the tobacco companies knew they were killing four million people throughout the world every year and making tens of millions more gravely ill. For fifty years the tobacco companies have known that cigarettes are addictive and give you cancer and have covered it up. They told us that cigarettes were healthy, that they relieved stress and prevented heart attacks! That was all the inspiration I needed. I knew then that I couldn't walk away from that knowledge. I'd grown up in Ireland over the last fifty years and knew from personal experience that their target area was pre-teenage children. It caused me to smoke when I was ten. I thought I was Humphrey Bogart!

In the early days, people didn't take the case very seriously but in October 1997 I issued the first proceedings in the High Court in Dublin. At the time, there was a little bit of litigation taking place in the US and I started receiving calls from America and talking to the media in world terms. Very quickly I had a couple of thousand people who wanted me to sue these tobacco companies on their behalf. We don't have class actions in Ireland so it was extremely time-consuming to deal with each individual case. I issued proceedings on behalf of 300 people and then reduced that number down to 17 test cases. I wasn't paid and to this day have not received any money for the work I do. I personally funded all the necessary medical reports, examinations and government duties. I became the European expert on tobacco and education. There was a firm in London called Leigh Day who were ahead of me by about two years in terms of litigation but their case collapsed. So I became the leading anti-tobacco lawyer in Europe. As far back as 35 years ago, Professor Dick Daynard, a law professor at North Eastern University, Boston started holding conferences because the US is the centre of the tobacco industry. I got invited to speak at these and have spoken all over the world. Each time, I had to pay for a team to come with me, put them up in a hotel, and fund the trip. I have invested so much time, emotion and money into this cause.

Sometimes I found myself wondering what on earth I was doing. Should I not be at home, earning a living for my family? But the simple answer is that I knew it was the right thing to do. In 1998, Phillip Morris finally admitted on their website that cigarettes might make you ill and they might be addictive! They knew they couldn't go into the new millennium without acknowledging this fact at least. So we started briefing Brian Cowen, then Minister for Health in Ireland. We told him and his department that if the state sued the tobacco companies for the crippling cost to healthcare, as was the case in the US, they would win. Their reaction was: Don't be so ridiculous – look at all the tax we get from these companies. The truth is: this tax comes from the citizens who buy tobacco, not from the companies that sell it, and the effects of smoking actually use up almost the entire health budget. We didn't give up and when Michael Martin, the new Minister for Health, came into power, he took the case seriously.

An all-party committee was formed; it produced an excellent report on the international effects of smoking. Their conclusion was that the Irish Government should definitely sue the tobacco industry. As a result of the report, the legal age to buy tobacco was raised from 16 to 18. The Government also set up the Office of Tobacco Control and brought in my agenda to ban smoking in the workplace. Ireland now leads the way in Europe. It has become a health and safety issue and effectively creates a total smoking ban in all public spaces. A lot of people are very grateful for this. Britain should have a complete ban too and stop messing about.

I've managed to persuade senior legal professionals over the years to help me battle against the big boys, free of charge. All you have to do is approach people with logic; convince them by appealing to their brain, gut and heart. The power and money working against us is frightening, usually around 100 of their lawyers against two of us. The multinational tobacco firms fund these lawyers on a monthly basis – we just spend money, with no income at all. The next stage is to get to the High Court and then on to the Supreme Court in Ireland. The fact that it's taken so long to get this far has been a good thing. The world is a wiser place now. Medicine, science and society have moved on. We need to get to court in about eighteen months' time. Now that the tobacco industry is being squeezed out of the developed world they are starting to concentrate on the developing world, in particular Africa, China and India. These companies are seriously powerful and influential, the world over. They give bursaries to scientists to say that cigarettes are actually good for your body. They lobby politicians and captains of industry. This can't be done openly any more but it still goes on. The sale of tobacco is legitimate yet it is the only legal substance sold on the open market that is bad for you no matter what. Their campaigns for ultra-low-tar brands are so devious. They are far worse for you than smoking an unfiltered Woodbine. It's very tiring for everyone involved in the anti-tobacco campaign but we won't let go because we know we're right.

Once we've won, I'll go around the world educating others to give them the ammunition to fight these tobacco companies and win. This is about changing the law worldwide. My father, a teacher, died at 86 having smoked since he was ten years old. He once joked that he would be a witness for the tobacco industry! But at 58, cigarettes almost killed him with a series of heart attacks so he took up alcohol for the first time in his life. He had two neat brandies and twenty cigars a day instead. I grew up among good people who made things happen. If we needed a school built, we'd raise the money and build it. We did what needed to be done. We weren't the kind to sit around and moan or wait for someone else or the state to sort it. The reason I chose law was because you can do something that will really make a difference to people's lives worldwide. And because of Perry Mason on the telly, of course!

On 29 March 2005, the first anniversary of the ban, the *Independent* newspaper quoted Bertie Ahern, the Irish Prime Minister, in declaring it an outstanding success: 'We can share a sense of national pride in a measure that will have significant health implications, not just for us here today, but for our children and generations to come.' He had good reason to be thrilled at the position of Ireland leading the world, but the truth is that if it hadn't been for one man inspiring and convincing government ministers of the need to take action, there would be nothing to celebrate today. As a lawyer, Peter McDonnell is trained to apply rigorous logic backed up with compelling facts and figures to win his cases and the evidence he presented to Ireland's Health Minister, Michael Martin, was irrefutable: tobacco is estimated to kill six times as many people in Ireland as road accidents, work accidents, drugs, murder, suicide and Aids combined, and is a massive drain on the nation's health service. 'All you have to do is approach people with logic; convince them by appealing to their brain, gut and heart.'

Sometimes inspiring others has to come from cold logic as well as inflamed passion. That is exactly the strategy employed by Peter McDonnell for nearly ten years. It was all the more remarkable when you think of the devastating personal stories he has come across during this time: lives cut short or destroyed by the effects of smoking. 'Money isn't the issue for any of my clients. It's just the only language tobacco companies understand. It's not some kind of money bandwagon. These people are angry and they want justice. They're not able to walk to the door, they've lost limbs, they've lost lungs.' One of his better-known clients is the legendary former world snooker champion, Alex 'Hurricane'

Higgins, who was sponsored by tobacco firms throughout his career and encouraged to chain-smoke on camera during tournaments. Alex is now desperately ill with throat cancer.

Peter McDonnell cuts an impressive figure. Sipping tea in one of London's smartest hotels, immaculately dressed in a Savile Row suit, he looks more like a wealthy Italian businessman than a passionate Irish lawyer. But as soon as he begins talking I can easily see how he could take on the world's tobacco giants and win. Later, I thought how interesting it would be to televise a debate between Peter and our world leaders, Tony Blair or George Bush, and see how they would defend their stance on the tobacco industry. Or with Tory MP Kenneth Clarke, the UK's former Chancellor and currently Deputy Chairman of British American Tobacco. Now that really would be interesting.

Inspire Yourself

The first thing Peter said about inspiration was, 'You have to keep yourself inspired before you can inspire anybody else.' Listening to him talk, I realised the importance of this if you are to stay motivated when the going gets tough. Many of the people he has known and represented will never have their day in court, having died painful deaths as a result of tobacco products. I was also aware of the financial strain he must have suffered, with so much of his time and energy devoted to a campaign that has never paid him a penny. Peter's response was simple: 'You just have to keep on reminding yourself why you're doing it. I know I will win. I have won great victories already and I know I'm right. I never seriously thought about giving up.'

Stay Motivated

If you can keep on reigniting your own inspiration, by referring back to your vision, you're much better placed to stay motivated.

Keep reminding yourself why you're doing what you're doing. Recall your original inspiration. Keep your vision clearly in mind. This is true for any goal or campaign. Refuel your inspiration along the way with the satisfaction of the small victories. Continuous applause will keep you buoyed up. Don't wait for the final big victory to celebrate. You've got to keep yourself going until then. The saying, 'Success breeds success' is absolutely true, but only when you notice that success can you feed off it. Pay attention to all your successes. Find reasons to be optimistic.

Take regular breaks. A ten-year campaign like Peter McDonnell's requires energy and stamina to sustain. It is vital to take time out to recharge and refresh yourself, otherwise you risk burn-out of the body and spirit. If you're to last the course, you mustn't feel guilty about stepping out and coming back reinvigorated. That's the way to build staying power.

Unlock Potential

There's one thing all inspiring people have in common: they are more alive, switched-on, vital and exciting than the average person. You can feed off their life force and feel your own spirit, enthusiasm and morale surge. You feel more is possible with these people and, of course, it's true. And we all want to be more like this ourselves, so being around them helps. Their magic rubs off. The greatest choreographer of the twentieth century, George Balanchine, was one such person. Here's what a favourite dancer said of him: 'No one who had even the briefest contact with him was left untouched; those who knew him well were changed for ever. Many people, on meeting him for the first time, expected to find a man full of false airs, but his disarming lack of pretension and his natural modesty made them feel more important in his presence.'

My work as a coach has brought me into contact with many other coaches over the years. There are those who do a perfectly good job and there are those who help people fulfil their deepest desires and dreams and become all that they are capable of, and more. These last are the coaches who know how to inspire and that's the secret of their success. I have also worked out with numerous fitness trainers myself and only one or two in over ten years ever spoke of my fabulous potential and the wonderful shape that was just waiting to reveal itself once a few layers had been shed. Only one ever held up the vision of my ideal look and got excited about it. The others just didn't rev up my enthusiasm and motivation, *and inspire me*.

When you want to inspire someone, map out a vision of their great, limitless, fabulous potential. Whether you're working to attain their ideal physical shape or life state, grasp the sight of their grandest version of themselves and empathise with them on its wondrous possibilities. Draw for them the picture of their perfection. Hold out the highest expectations for them and genuinely expect them to fulfil them. One of the greatest gifts you can give another person is to spot their potential, however dormant, and shine some light on it for them. Think of yourself as a talent scout, looking for the greatness and genius lurking, untapped, within people. Focus on helping them fulfil their objectives. Ensure that you want what they want as much as they want it themselves and you'll automatically fulfil your own potential as well and be one of the most sought-after trainers or coaches that you know!

Ensure that your presence inspires others to greatness and, above all, choose to trust. Be generous and look for generosity in others, anticipating goodwill. Empathise and understand the other person's position and priorities. Always be optimistic. Build people up. Maintain an upbeat outlook and can-do manner that engages and draws people to you. Keep yourself in good spirits so you are quite simply immensely attractive and positively irresistible!

* * *

One lady who is definitely all of the above is the impossibly glamorous theatre mogul, Sally Greene. Sally is one of the most photographed women in London and New York and her spirit shines through every photo I've ever seen of her, even when she's standing next to Bill Clinton or a major Hollywood star! Arguably the best-connected woman in London, and probably beyond, she is England's most influential theatre impresario.

Sally Greene is most renowned for rescuing London's Old Vic theatre, persuading Kevin Spacey to divert from a Hollywood career and take over as artistic director and filling the board with power players. She has also entirely redeveloped the Richmond Theatre and the Criterion Theatre. She's a governor of the Royal Shakespeare Company, a director of the Manchester Royal Exchange and a renowned producer, with shows in the West End, on national tour and on Broadway. She's just taken over London's legendary jazz club, Ronnie Scott's, and has produced the *Billy Elliot* musical (with music by her friend Elton John) and *The Vagina Monologues* with Sharon Osborne. And she's involved with countless charities, including one run by another pal, Hillary Clinton.

Sally Greene

I love the fact that I inspire people. It's key to everything I've achieved. I was recently on a flight from LA and this stranger, who turned out to be a very successful man in the entertainment industry, said: 'When I looked at you I noticed a glow and just wanted to talk to you, find out what you did, how you made it work.' You can't have inhibitions about talking to people. I have never been nervous about meeting anyone. When I was younger, apparently, I always went up to people, would look them in the eye and ask them pertinent questions.

My dream is never just about the show but also about

creating a whole atmosphere around it: the theatre, the building, the people in it. People feel a big spark when they come to work at the Old Vic. They are lit up in some way; they're special and feel part of it. It's got to be everyone together. I never say someone works for me, they work with me.

A lot of people follow other people's dreams and feed off that energy. They don't harness it for themselves. But it's only your dream that's going to get you into the successful place you want to be. I had a dream in my head about theatre and followed that. Of course, some days I doubt the whole thing, there are definitely days like that. But I have always believed that if I have a really bad day or week, then the next one will be much better. I tend to think good follows bad, not bad follows bad. Energy and enthusiasm are contagious.

I am definitely an optimist. Living with a mother who was a manic-depressive was difficult, but I remember thinking I'd never be like her – she always had the lights off, never saw sunshine, there was no fire at Christmas. I'm the total opposite. I said to myself when I was a little girl: I'm never going to feel 'the black Irish Depression' as my dad called it. My father was an optimist and I don't know how he managed it either. In those days post-natal depression was rarely diagnosed. My mother suffered from it after having all four of her children. She died of cancer four years ago and it was only then that I discovered she'd been on lithium for years. I read an article the other day that said that optimists aren't really as successful as pessimists because pessimists expect the worst and are better prepared for it, so are therefore more realistic. What a load of bollocks!

I've just taken twenty of our top investors to the Oscars and Elton John's party. I knew that's what they really wanted and I can deliver that through my contacts in the theatre. I have a feeling for what people want. Having a production company, I entertain them. I take them to parties. When I first started out with the Richmond Theatre it was falling apart physically and artistically. It needed someone to nurture it, get it back together and raise the necessary funds. During that time I started to understand how important it was to get the right people on board to help you. Friends have stuck with me even when the odds looked insurmountable. In 1998 I wandered round the Old Vic shaking my head – miserable, wrong side of the tracks, covered in litter and with a history of financial failure – and thinking that whoever took the place on would have to be mad. But I knew there and then that I wanted to take it on and I believed that I could bring people with me. It was tough. I did a lot of talking it up to others. I had to raise £1.5 million in three months and a further £2 million to be paid over two years. I sat down with my address book and telephone and got so stressed that I went to my own opening night with viral meningitis. But I did it.

I would say I am generous to a fault and definitely give too much. I just love talking to people with ideas and I do genuinely like to help people younger than me who are on the way up. I tend to keep away from people with cobwebs around them – if they haven't had a fresh idea for a while, I'm not interested.

I don't want to give up and would like to go on until I die. I would like to make a movie of a theatre musical, something that really touches me, and I'd like to have another couple of theatres. I am terribly, terribly passionate about what I do. I love the immediacy of it and that I can make a difference straight away. I can put a big musical like Billy Elliot *together within a matter of months. I love that.*

Talking to Sally is like being injected with a shot of adrenalin. She talks fast, and you want to hang on to every word. She is utterly comfortable in her own skin, and with every type of person. She's not thrown by royalty, Hollywood legends, presidents or prime ministers. That alone makes her very easy for these power brokers to be around. There's nothing fake or fawning about her, which allows for genuine friendship to develop. To be a successful and influential networker, you've got to exude loads of personal confidence and sheer chutzpah. This was her response the moment she met her husband, property tycoon Robert Bourne, on a blind date: 'I realised what he needed was me.' Don't you just love that? This was at a tricky time for her as well. Her acting career wasn't working and her lover had just left her to marry someone else. That's the sort of self-esteem we all want and admire in others when we see it, because it's so exceptional. It's just so audacious!

The key thing to take from Sally Greene, as from Peter McDonnell, is that to inspire others you must first be inspired yourself. Sally took on the Old Vic even though it was in a desperate state because she was inspired by its potential. Once she was fired up, she *knew* she could inspire others to feel the same way and share her dream of restoring it to its former glory. In this she echoes the message of Carmel McConnell: you succeed in your goals by first helping other people achieve theirs. A shared vision with everyone wanting the same dream is crucial to the success of any venture. You can't impose inspiration on others, you can't pay people to feel it, but you can ignite it in them. This reinforces my father's words of wisdom, quoted at the beginning of the chapter: 'The best way to get someone to do something is to get them to *want* to do it.' I don't believe you can do this in a contrived, insincere way. I believe the sincerity and depth of your own inspiration are essential to successfully inspiring others.

The more noble and worthwhile your vision, the more inspired people will be by it. If you are running an organisation and your vision is to make a personal fortune, you are unlikely to *really* inspire others with that vision, even if they stand to benefit financially themselves. What is more likely to inspire them is knowing they are achieving something truly valuable through coming to work each day. The incredible success of

Emma Harrison's business is proof of this. When they have their annual conference, they don't sit around figuring out how to make more money. They talk about the expansion of their 'one vision', and ways to spread their work internationally to improve even more people's lives. Now, that's inspiring.

Whether you want to feed hungry children, end unemployment, challenge multinationals in the courts, be a brilliant theatre impresario or simply lead the most successful life possible for you, you need other people to help you do it – you need to be able to inspire others. Use the wisdom, apply the strategies and follow the examples of the foregoing case studies. Become adept at inspiring others, make the world a more interesting place and watch your vision grow.

I have always been inspired by what Robert Kennedy said when he pointed out that all great progress is the accumulation of individual acts.

> It is from the numberless diverse acts of courage and belief that human history is shaped. Each time a man stands up for an ideal, or acts to improve the lot of others, or strikes out against injustice, he sends a tiny ripple of hope, and crossing each other from a million different centres of energy and daring, those ripples build a current which can sweep down the mightiest walls of oppression and resistance.

He said that in 1966. Forty years later his words are more powerful than ever.

Five Steps to Inspire Others

1. Be optimistic and enthusiastic. Charge yourself up with enthusiasm for life and what you do. People can't help but notice you when you glow with energy and excitement. Ensure that you are one of life's energisers and uplifters. Sprinkle a little magic dust over people at every opportunity.

2. Embolden yourself. Everyone loves a confident leader. Avoid ambivalence and indecision. Command attention with certainty and conviction. No obstacle can overwhelm you, as you stretch to contain it. Manage bouts of self-doubt without infecting others with it.

3. Have a vision. Have your own dream, a higher purpose. Everyone should have in their life something bigger than themselves. If there isn't the sublime and noble somewhere in the picture, then there's something missing. Invite others to join you on your mission. Never make it about the money. It's *always* about the vision.

4. Empathise. Empathise. Empathise. Understand what people want and ensure they get it when they join your team. Create the circumstances for people to fulfil themselves and be happy. Help people to get the best out of themselves. Choose to trust them.

5. Stay inspired. Keep your own spark in good shape. Don't get dull and run-down. Stay focused on your vision but take time off to renew and recharge your batteries often. Have fun. Enjoy life. No matter how worthy your vision, don't take the shine off it by getting tired or over-serious. Keep it light!

6: *Persevere*

There's a saying that when the going gets tough, the tough get going. There's another one: 'Expect the best and prepare for the worst.' There's a lot of truth in both of them. What they are really suggesting is, tough times happen, difficulties, disappointments, disasters, too. This might sound obvious but the people who really grasp this reality and deal with it well are exceptional. It's easy to pay lip service to this truth but applying it and living with it are something else altogether. In reality, many people fall at the first hurdle and flounder when things don't go exactly to plan. One of the untruest sayings is that the first step is the hardest. That's nonsense. It's really the fourth, fifth and twenty-fifth that are the hardest, once the initial excitement has calmed down. The simple truth is, people who succeed are those who have persevered.

Contemporary culture tells us otherwise. It gives us airbrushed images of perfection, success and happiness that look like they're totally effortless. If you're not careful, you could begin to think that there's something seriously wrong if your success isn't happening overnight. But the most enduring overnight successes have taken years to achieve. Look at the actress they're calling 'the Queen of Hollywood'. Catherine Zeta-Jones may have been crowned overnight but she's been working all her life for the title. She joined her local dance school at five, which means it's actually taken her thirty-two years to become Queen! By the time she was ten, she had already sung and danced her way to local stardom in Wales and at 14 headed to London to audition for, and win, a part in *Bugsy Malone*. She's worked long and hard to get to where she is. Interestingly, she could have had a much easier life if she had agreed to marry Hollywood producer Jon Peters in 1992. She refused, saying she didn't want to be just a 'Hollywood wife'.

It's the same story for 'the Queen of Pop', Madonna, and 'the Princess of Pop', Kylie Minogue. They have both worked their socks off for their titles from an early age, handling career dips, regular criticism and personal setbacks when they occurred. Neither is thought to be the most talented singer or dancer in the world, but dogged determination has made up for any shortfall and they reign supreme. It's not necessarily the most talented who win through; it's the most determined. The world of showbiz, like every other world, is full of talented people who'll never make it because talent is no substitute for staying power. Those who reach the top do so because they have the muscle and grit to keep going, recover, make changes and keep going some more. Their determination, usually described as 'ruthless', takes them far.

Often, when success comes too easily or too early, it doesn't last. We can feel we haven't really earned it, or we lack the experience and depth of wisdom to handle it or truly appreciate it. The message is: Stop expecting things to be easy – and fast. If they sometimes are, take it as a bonus. We live in a quick-fix, fast-food world where we're conditioned to want it all, right here, right now, yesterday if possible. But real life and lasting success is not like that. Here's another saying: 'If it's worth having, it's worth working for.' In other words, be prepared to put the work in and keep putting it in. Persevere.

I've brought four fascinating people to the table here. Each one is completely different from the others in terms of their life experiences and challenges. But you cannot read their words without being touched by the power of their perseverance. The capacity to pick yourself up after a setback or push yourself to keep going beyond the limit of what you think you can achieve is vital for success in every area of your life, from working for a promotion to running in a marathon to writing that novel you've been planning. Michelle Mone's story of determination and persistence illustrates that perfectly.

Michelle grew up fast, developing her perseverance muscle when she set up a business in the competitive and highly lucrative lingerie industry. In 1996, at the age of 24, as a mother in Glasgow, Michelle dreamt up a revolutionary bra which created a high-street sensation. Her gel-filled bra used moulded silicone of the kind used in breast-enhancement operations to give a cleavage that was comfortable, and convincing, unlike any other bra on the market. Three years later the Ultimo went into production and is now sold in stores across the world. Its launch in New York's prestigious Saks department store racked up a six-week waiting list. Sales have now broken the £10-million barrier and Ultimo products are on the verge of going global.

Michelle left school at 15 to go out to work and look after her father when he woke up one day to find himself paralysed. Her home in the 'tough east end' of Glasgow didn't have a bath until she was 12. She went on to become marketing director for Labatts lager, covering all of Scotland, until redundancy enabled her to start her own business. But her dream came at a high price, putting at risk her health and her marriage and ultimately, even her personal safety.

Michelle Mone

Had I known the truth about the lingerie industry when I started out nearly ten years ago, I would certainly have thought twice about what I was letting myself in for. The word 'lingerie' conjures up images of beautifully buxom young women, their curves clad in lace, but the reality is that this is a male-dominated industry where dirty tricks, back-stabbing and industrial espionage are rife.

One evening back in 1995 I was at a dinner-dance and was wearing a well-known make of cleavage-enhancing bra. It was so uncomfortable that I had to take it off. I remember thinking, 'There must be a comfortable bra out there that can give me a cleavage and not feel as if it's killing me.' That night I told my husband Michael that I wanted to design a bra that would fit properly. I had recently been made redundant from my job with a brewery company and was in the fortunate position of having £15,000 to finance my dream. I funded the research and worked with a team of scientists to find a substance which would mimic breast tissue. Michael kept his job going for three years which allowed us to form MJM International, working from the bedroom of our house. To survive, we took out a second mortgage and lived off credit cards. It was touch and go – until the day in 1999 when the Ultimo bra went on sale at Selfridges.

That was my real breakthrough. I was interviewed on radio that morning by Chris Evans on his breakfast show and he asked me what I'd do if the bra wasn't successful. 'My house will go to the wall,' I told him. And I wasn't kidding, even though I'd just had my third child, Bethany. At that time I was about £35,000 in debt because I was sinking everything into the business and I'd put my house up for security. But when we got to Selfridges, people were queuing around the block. The store said they'd never seen anything like it; we sold out in under two hours. It was an instant and huge success and quickly became one of the country's biggest-selling cleavage-enhancing bras. It was worn by Julia Roberts in the Oscar-winning film, Erin Brockovich, *and soon other actresses and celebrities 'came out' as fans and everyone was talking about it. The press loved it.*

But our success alerted our competitors to what they were missing out on. Suddenly other firms saw us as a threat, and things got really nasty. The first problem came in 2002 when a big-name UK brand took umbrage at our success. Annoyed by the design awards we were winning and the publicity we enjoyed, they decided to try to sink us. They began legal proceedings against us on the grounds that our name was similar to theirs – in fact the two names are nothing like each other – and took out an injunction forcing us to remove our products from stores nationwide.

It was a clever move. Industry giants can afford to be locked into costly legal wrangling for months and they thought this would send us under. They expected us to be off the shop floor for at least three months while we created new packaging, but to their surprise we had our new packaging delivered to every store in the UK within a week. I even delivered some to stores myself.

When you stand up to bullies they invariably back off and it's the same in business. When the company involved saw the lengths we were prepared to go to to protect our brand, they dropped proceedings. We were safe for the moment, but we'd had a serious wake-up call.

Later that year came the event which nearly sank us completely. After careful research we were due to break into the American market. It was an exciting time – I'd been courted by all the major department stores and the president of Saks Fifth Avenue had even phoned me to ask for the product. It seemed we were on the brink of major stateside success. I was determined to get things right and took pains to choose a good distributor, finally settling on a firm who came highly recommended by the top industry trade magazine. My trust proved horribly misplaced. The company went bust and the owners ran off with almost £250,000 of our money, leaving us with a warehouse of stock we couldn't shift because it was the previous season's design. My American dreams were dashed and because of our losses we were forced to refinance the company using our house as security. I also discovered that the distributor had gone bust several times before and that the editor of the magazine was a personal friend of theirs.

At the time, I thought my world had collapsed. If I hadn't had my family I'd have gone insane. Some marriages might not have survived the strain, and we have certainly had our difficult times but thankfully we have ended up stronger than ever.

Even once we'd recouped our losses after a year, the troubles were not over. Our sales were dropping alarmingly. Research showed that this was because people were ripping off our product and producing inferior look-alikes at much cheaper prices. We didn't have the money to fight back with injunctions, so it took its toll. We decided to put America on hold, to withdraw from all the department stores in the UK and concentrate on expanding our portfolio of designs. I turned my attention to designing the next invention, the 'backless body'. The design was patented worldwide in 2002 at a cost of tens of thousands and went on to become a massive best-seller. Then, shortly before we launched, I had a call from a colleague telling me that a major UK retailer had an identical body in their stores. It was the same in every way: cut, material, everything.

Once again, an industry giant didn't think I had the money, time or energy to fight them off, but this time I decided to begin legal proceedings. When they saw I meant business they settled out of court and removed their copy from the shelves. As if these dirty tricks weren't bad enough, in February 2003 I was loading my car outside my office with £30,000 of samples of new designs when a hooded man grabbed me and threatened me with a knife before driving off in my car. I struggled for as long as I could – the loss of those prototypes could have meant the end of our business as each one can take six months to put together – and received bruises and a cracked rib in the process. The car was found by the police, but the underwear had gone.

The police never got to the bottom of it, but industrial espionage was the first thing which crossed my mind. After all, the thief had stolen a £54,000 BMW only to dump it, but had taken the samples of underwear. It was all very suspicious. Every one of those designs was a one-off so we had to work twenty-four hours a day for a week to remake the samples. Again we were lucky to survive. I put out a statement saying it was 'business as usual at MJM'.

I've got to stay strong as we've got three young children to care for and I've staked everything I have on the business. I'm not prepared just to roll over and let my rivals win. I have learnt some harsh lessons and, although I would call myself determined rather than ruthless, I've really had to toughen up and realise that I can't trust people so readily. As long as my family, friends and staff know what I'm like, I can deal with the rest.

And I always come back stronger and more determined. The knocks strengthen me. The BBC filmed us for two years, and the programme has been shown in forty countries and I got thousands of emails and letters of support following it. For the last five years I have been on the board of the Prince's Trust in Scotland. It's important to me to inspire young people from backgrounds like mine to aim high. But I would warn any kid starting out in business: never think it can happen to you overnight. You have to put everything you've got on the line to make it work. You've got to be determined and if you don't want it 120 per cent, don't try.

As long as you've got determination and focus in life you will succeed. We have won scores of awards and accolades, including Business of the Year, and I have been voted Businesswoman of the Year. The press say I'm the female Richard Branson. I had supper with Anita Roddick last night; now she is an incredible woman. I'm sick and tired of all the successful people in business being men. Not all, but a lot of them, look down on me and think, 'Who the hell is she?' In business I am the most confident person in the world. I feel I can take any of them on any day. I thrive on that: them trying to put me down, thinking that I must be stupid. Oh, I love a challenge!

There will always be competition and people out to knock us. I've just got to live with that. As long as I can say I've had a go and done something with my life, I'll be happy. You can't put down a trier.

I was introduced to the Ultimo by my friend Carole, who had a lingerie mail-order business. We knew it was a winner and would be sensationally successful. Over the next few weeks, we watched the media frenzy unfold. All the press had their own take on this incredible invention. I knew that Michelle Mone was incredibly smart not only to have created the Ultimo, but to be able to take it to market in this way. Over the years I've kept an eye on the trials that she has faced, from competitors' lawsuits and press snipes to the occasion when she was attacked and all thirty of her new designs stolen. So, I was eager to spend time with her and hear for myself how she had weathered these storms.

The one thing that really struck me about Michelle was that this girl had fabulous backbone. I knew I was talking to someone who would never be beaten. Her glamorous, blonde, model-girl appearance belies the tough strategist that she actually is. Some will call her ruthless, or worse. I see it as the most awesome clarity and determination. As long as she knows she is right and her cause justified, she'll go full steam ahead to win through. Perhaps we're just not comfortable seeing this in a woman? In a man, we admire it – it's called 'having balls'! I suspect that leaving school at 15 to be the breadwinner would kick-start the sort of drive and resilience you just don't see in the average teenager.

One thing that Michelle's story illustrates perfectly is that once you make waves and are visibly successful, whether in gaining nationwide publicity or getting fast-track promotion, you must be prepared for criticism and personal attacks. Reaffirming who you are and knowing the truth of the matter is vital. Remembering that you can never please all the people all the time lets you know who is important in your life. As Michelle said, 'So long as my family, friends and staff know what I'm like, I can deal with the rest.' With that sort of clarity, you make yourself invincible. Whatever the opposition throws at you, you'll handle it, or let it slide right off you. And the challenge is not just to survive, but to come through with your spirit uncrushed and intact. F. Scott Fitzgerald put it well when he said, 'Vitality shows in not only the ability to persist but the ability to start over.'

Expect the Best

Michelle may not have been prepared for the worst but she certainly expected the best. Without this fundamental optimism, it's hard to start anything new. More importantly, without it, you're more likely to give up at the fourth or fifth hurdle. After all, hard work for no reward is not in our definition of success. So you need to feel that your perseverance has a positive goal, that you expect to see results. Michelle seems to have been blessed with an inbuilt faith which grew stronger as she needed it. This basic confidence in yourself and your abilities is reflected in your willingness to persevere with challenges and shows up at an early age. In his best-selling book, *Emotional Intelligence*, Daniel Goldman recounts the work of eminent Harvard paediatrician Dr T. Berry Brazelton. Dr Brazelton has a simple test of a baby's basic outlook on life. He offers two blocks to an eight-month-old, then shows the baby how he wants her to put the two blocks together. A baby who is hopeful about life, who has confidence in her own abilities, will pick up one block, mouth it, rub it in her hair and drop it over the side of the table to see whether you will retrieve it for her. When you do, she finally completes the requested task – placing the two blocks together. Then she gazes at you with a bright-eyed look of expectancy that says, 'Tell me how great I am!' Babies like these have enjoyed healthy approval and encouragement from the adults around them; they expect to succeed in life's challenges. By contrast, babies who have been ignored and neglected go about the same task in a way that signals they already expect to fail. Even as they complete it their demeanour is 'hangdog', as if to say, 'I'm no good. See, I've failed.' Such children are likely to go through life with a defeatist attitude.

Optimism means having a strong expectation that, in general, things will turn out all right, despite setbacks and frustrations. It's an attitude that sustains you through tough times, protecting you from resignation, hopelessness, depression or apathy. In his book, *Learned Optimism*, the psychologist Martin Seligman refers to a study of insurance salesmen with the MetLife company, which provides a telling demonstration of the power of optimism to motivate people and keep them going. Telephone sales has one of the highest drop-out rates of any job, with three-quarters of salesmen quitting in their first three years. By the second year of the experiment the optimists were outselling the pessimists by 57 per cent. And during the first year the pessimists quit at twice the rate of the optimists.

Check Your Attitude

As with any other attitude, optimism can be learnt and enhanced. It's interesting to take note of your early influences and conditioning, but in no way are you, or do you have to be, determined by it. Why not take a few minutes to pinpoint what you have picked up about yourself, your abilities and your potential?

Simply finish off the following statements, so that you're in no doubt about this and can see if you need to review or revamp your approach.

What's Your Attitude?

Complete the following statements with the first thing that comes to mind. Complete each statement five times.

Something I learnt from my father about me was I'm . . .

Something I learnt from my father about life was . . .

Something I learnt from my mother about me was I'm . . .

Something I learnt from my mother about life was . . .

And what I believe about me that holds me back is . . .

What I wish I believed is . . .

And the attitude that would really empower me is . . .

Take as long as you want to review the information. The really important statements are the last two. These are the beliefs you want to build on and build into your outlook and modus operandi. Over time, and surprisingly quickly, they'll become true for you and bring results. Our aim is to engender the feeling that you have mastery over the events of your life and can meet challenges as they come up: an outlook psychologists call self-efficacy.

Albert Bandura, a Stanford psychologist who has carried out much of the research on self-efficacy, puts it like this: 'People's beliefs about their abilities have a profound effect on those abilities. Ability is not a fixed property; there is a huge variability in how you perform. People who have a sense of self-efficacy bounce back from failures; they approach things in terms of how to handle them rather than worrying about what can go wrong.'

I've already emphasised under Rule 4: **Take More Risks**, the importance of not making *yourself* the failure when things go wrong, but of dispassionately assessing the situation. The message we're seeing here is: an optimistic resilience underpins perseverance. And one of the greatest threats to that attitude is condemning yourself as a failure, especially before you've even started! Remember, neither beliefs nor ability are fixed.

Persevere Optimistically and Live Longer

Life's better when you're an optimist. It's not about being a fool and closing your eyes to the facts around you. It's about knowing that you'll manage, find a way to win through. You'll handle it. Even if you feel you aren't naturally an optimist, put the work in to nudge yourself over into this category. You can do it. I've coached numerous people to change their thinking. It can, and must, be done! If you need further convincing, take a look at all the research that keeps telling us that optimists live longer than people who have a bleak outlook on life. An often-quoted study is the one carried out at the Mayo Clinic in Minnesota where scientists studied 839 patients over forty years and concluded that optimists have a 19 per cent longer lifespan. Jibby Beane, whom we'll meet shortly, is living proof that perseverance combined with optimism produces quality and quantity of life.

Optimists are more likely to look after their health. Additionally, having a positive attitude helps the immune system fight disease, warding off the ageing process. And people who fight disease with a stubborn defiance often live longer than those who just give up.

Carry on Persevering, However Old You Are

Sometimes success later in life is better. This is certainly the view of ex-actor Ron McLarty who became an overnight sensation at fifty-six with his book, *The Memory of Running*. For years Ron used to spend his days writing books and plays – in longhand in his basement. He would then have them typed up and post them off to publishers, who rarely responded. Thirty years later he had the satisfaction of seeing those same literary giants scrabbling to sign him up for 'obscene' amounts of money: a reported £1 million two-book deal with Penguin Putnam in the US and Time Warner in the UK. 'Now they were telling me they loved me, that I was a genius. At a certain age you have an overview of things. If I'd had this good fortune when I was 26 instead of 56, I might have been overawed, but now I can appreciate it for what it is. You understand everything better when you are older and you enjoy things more.'

The Memory of Running is being filmed by Alfonso Cuarón who directed the latest Harry Potter film. Interestingly, Ron was spurred into writing it by the death of his parents in a car crash: 'I didn't want to curl up with a bottle of vodka.' Unable to get it published, he struck a deal with a talking-books publisher to put his acting skills to good use and record his book in exchange for his reading a few other books for free. One and a half years later Stephen King listened to *Running* and described it as 'a book than can do more than walk; it has a chance to be a breakout best-seller'. The rest, as they say, is history.

Ron McLarty's perseverance was incredible. For many years he received no encouragement from anyone. His family jokingly referred to his writing den as 'the pit of despair'. 'Publishers didn't even send my manuscripts back, and I always sent a stamped addressed envelope.' Even when there was no audience Ron still wrote, from 5 until 10 a.m.: 'I never tired of writing, even though friends often said that they thought I was nuts. Incidentally, my work wasn't always ignored – sometimes publishers sent rejection slips, which I stuck to the ceiling.'

It can also take time to grow into the most polished version of yourself. Franklin D. Roosevelt was one of America's most popular presidents, the only man in US politics to be elected President a third and fourth time, in the 1940 and 1944 elections. He was a great speaker and was able to give the impression that he enjoyed meeting the people and shaking their hands. He had 'the common touch'. But in his early days he wasn't so impressive, seemed overly serious, awkward and not particularly charming. One colleague, who later served in his government, remembers, 'No one who saw him in those years would have been likely to think of him as a potential president of the USA.' In 1921 Roosevelt was crippled with polio. Recovery was slow and tremendously hard work. He fought back and in 1928 became Governor of New York and President in 1932. His wife, Eleanor, gave an intriguing insight into the changes that had taken place within him, turning him into the charismatic, much-loved leader he became:

> Perhaps the experience, above all others, which shaped my husband's character and gave him a strength and a depth he did not have as a young man was the long struggle with polio. A strength of character was built up during those

days which made him able to give complete confidence to the people of the nation when they needed it, so that when he said, 'the only thing we have to fear is fear itself', they knew he believed it. He had lived through fear and come out successfully.

It's Never Too Late to Succeed

One person whose story totally illustrates the amazing power of optimism, as well as its link with longevity, is Jibby Beane. Jibby changed her life around by taking an audacious risk but her self-belief and her innate optimism meant she was fully equipped to succeed, even though she was 50 when she reinvented herself. Perseverance underpins the sense that it's never too late to succeed.

Jibby Beane pioneered the trend of selling art in a domestic setting in 1993. Until then, art was rigidly displayed in a formal gallery environment and young artists struggled to show their work. Jibby launched the careers of numerous artists by providing a gallery space, exposure and advice. With no formal training, she has made waves in the art world by buying and promoting artists she admires. At her peak, she was known as the Queen of London's art scene: no gallery opening, nightclub, disco or fashion show was complete without her. Before launching herself into London life in 1993 as she turned 50, she had been Mrs Mavis Norma Jane Beane, a housewife in Surrey, living in a £500,000 home, married to Ken and mother to Oliver and Henrietta. She swapped a secure and luxurious lifestyle for a new life in a little flat and a 24-year-old boyfriend.

Jibby Beane

I certainly wasn't the typical housewife. Even within my marriage, I always did my own thing. During that period, I was buying and selling houses while attending Richmond College, doing life-drawing classes, and then I took a fine arts course at 47.

I got into buying, refurbishing and selling the houses that we lived in, doing around sixteen altogether. Then various friends asked me to do the same for them and soon I had a business on the go. When the housing market took a downturn, I went to work for a friend in the Design and Decoration Building, which was a base for a lot of designers, in Pimlico. Among the various people working from there was Vivienne Westwood who I bumped into one day in the ladies' toilet. I told her how I had admired her from afar, not just her clothes but her joie de vivre. *She is very much her own person like myself. There was a connection between us and she invited me to work in her shop two days a week.*

Working for Vivienne Westwood in Conduit Street was like going on stage. It was just such a wonderful privilege, the dressing up, so theatrical, always an event. The spirit of her clothes so reflected my spirit – she dared to do. And so, at 51, I found myself on the catwalk alongside Naomi Campbell and Kate Moss! I felt reborn. It was during that period that I met an extraordinary young artist called Jonathan, who was 24, and proved to be a tremendous inspiration to me. I was going through a soul-searching time. He would read me Beckett and Joyce in his lunch hour. It was exciting. I had been so wrapped up in my husband and children over the years and was now hungry for it all. I left my husband, and went to live with my boyfriend, which was incredibly intellectually, spiritually and sexually stimulating.

I packed my belongings into six carrier bags and moved into his flat. It was back to one room but I felt I was getting in touch with myself. I had discussed it with my children first. An art critic friend of mine reminded me that before I had children, I promised myself I would be the very best mother I could be – and you know what, I think I was and still am. I'm so close to them. The twenty-seven years of marriage weren't all bad – we had some wonderful times but I felt spiritually I was dying. At the time my friends thought I was menopausal – it wasn't about that. It was about me, and one life. I wanted to feel the essence of what I was about. So I just did it. I'm sure a lot of people thought I was totally off the planet, but frankly I didn't care. Life is not a rehearsal, this is the real thing. I did not want to arrive at 60 or 70 and think, 'What have I done with my life?'

My interest in art up until then had been quite traditional. But I so loved Jonathan's work. It was geometric and mathematical. I found it tremendously inspirational. This young artist was introducing me to contemporary life, art and literature. He was feeding my soul. I spent the next two years developing my eye. What occurred to me was that there were a lot of brilliant young artists out there whose work simply wasn't getting seen.

It came to me in the middle of the night. By then I had moved to a flat in Bayswater. I thought: this is my home and, for the first time ever, I can do what I want, how I want. So I put on a show for my boyfriend, inviting about seventy people. Richard Dyer, the wonderful art critic and writer, telephoned me the next day to ask who I was showing next. Of course I didn't have a clue, but I'd been to all the graduate shows so I just went for people I liked. He wrote an article in the International Art News *about my concept of exhibiting art in a domestic setting which hadn't been done before. It just seemed to me that it was a chicken-and-egg situation. No one was giving these graduates a show until they'd had a show. So I began offering a platform for young artists in my apartment. I was quite maverick and radical about it. They had a 'gallery' to display their work and I got them the exposure. They had carte blanche to do whatever they wanted and the deal was fifty-fifty. It was a wonderful experience for me because I was actually living with the art and it was feeding my creativity.*

I want to be interesting to me. Amongst my interests is live and performance art. I wanted to bring the flavour of Greenwich

Village to London so decided to start an arts club. I began putting on various concerts in my flat until it became so popular that I needed to use other venues and consequently Adornments in St James's became my first arts club offering a platform to performance artists. We also had one-night art shows. I continued to put on a few salons in my home, showcasing various operas, and I did a year at Black's club in Soho, running a weekly salon which I really enjoyed too. I was surrounded by tremendous energy.

In 1996, I put on a show called Don't Be Scared, *addressing the Aids issue with Tony Kaye, the biggest commercials director in the world, in an 8000-square-foot space in Clerkenwell. I really forced him to do it and he flew over from LA with three men and three women who were all HIV positive. These brave individuals sat naked on the sofa, chatting to the thousands of people who came over three weeks. They had the most inspiring, optimistic outlook on life. It was emotionally draining but so powerful that I had grown men, City types, crying and incredibly moved. Critics and other artists said, 'But Jibby, where's the aesthetic?' but I took no notice. I then moved to this loft apartment above that space, hoping to turn it into a revolutionary venture – it was going to be a gallery, shop, café and arts club, open from 8 a.m. to 8 p.m. seven days a week, and I would live upstairs. It was a £1.5 million project and I had the backers, but at the eleventh hour they pulled out. That was incredibly disappointing, but you just have to pick yourself up and move on.*

In 2000 I had split up with Jonathan, who had been a tremendous force in my life. We had worked as a wonderful team but by then he was 34 and wanted marriage and children. So I was living on my own for the first time in my life and still dealing with art. Following stomach pains during a Royal Academy dinner, I was admitted to hospital with eight gallstones! I had never been in hospital in my life but was philosophical about it. I saw it as a holiday. A year before I had done a centre-fold for this magazine called Bare, *which I showed to my surgeon, saying, 'No scars please,' so he agreed to keyhole surgery. But they discovered cancerous cells in my colon and ten days later I had another operation to remove the cancer.*

The night before I went in for the operation, I attended five events – it was actually reported in the Daily Telegraph. *I was in intensive care for five days. I wasn't in denial but I didn't want my friends around. I thought: Jibby – you deal with it. Science has proved that how you deal with cancer in your head is crucial. I was warned that I would be depressed but I wasn't at all. I just saw that catching it in time was a gift. It was a short sharp shock and it made me be still.*

I've changed – my commitment now is utterly to me. I just let it all go, including dealing with artists. I realised it's about spending time alone and going within – happiness isn't all out there. In around nine years, I'd say I put on ninety-five events in London, New York and LA. I've got ten full press books – it just keeps coming. And even now, at 64, I'm with Models One agency, have done a lot of television and public speaking, including travelling to China for the British Council. When I spoke at a symposium of two hundred surgeons recently, I asked for a seat – not because I'm geriatric but because I had six-inch heels on, darling!

*Now I'm madly in love again, with Ernst, a 55-year-old artist, philosopher and writer, and while we spend huge chunks of time together, I also love my own space. I love living on my own. I'm 64 going on 24. Age is just a label. Now I'm looking for fresh challenges, a television show, my autobiography and a beauty campaign. I have to work. I keep going because I f***ing have to! And you know what – I am so happy to be me. We are all on this planet to realise our magnificence. Vive la différence, hey. I've been very much a free thinker all my life. If people call me a sensationalist, I have only one thing to say to them: 'So what? Who cares? Enjoy!'*

* * *

I had been intrigued by Jibby Beane ever since she first burst on to the London social scene fifteen years ago. She seemed to have come from nowhere and suddenly she was Vivienne Westwood's new model, running a gallery from her white Bayswater flat and spotting new talent in London's 'Brit Art' community. The press loved her: she was fresh and original. The fact that until recently she had been a suburban housewife only added to the fascination. There was just no one like her. Meeting her in the flesh was no disappointment. She looked simply amazing, larger than life in every way, from her Westwood stilettos, thick dyed blonde hair piled on top of her head and voluptuous mouth to her gregarious personality and grand spirit. Drinking tea in her minimalist loft apartment, I felt I had entered another world, Jibby's world.

Beyond her beauty, her spirit made her appear ageless. It felt as fresh, vital and optimistic as a 20-year-old's, the spark not dimmed or disappointed by the years. I had always known that she had to have a remarkable appetite for life to throw up a comfortable home for something utterly unknown in middle age. But what I didn't know was the real history and depth behind the glamorous image and glitzy lifestyle. Her decision to grab life and squeeze every bit of juice out of it was born from awareness, at a very young age, that life was down to what she did with it and made of it. Her early ambition was to be a dancer. Dame Ninette de Valois accepted her for the Royal Ballet, but her mother couldn't afford it. 'I realised early on that I had to take care of myself – and get over life's knocks.'

Jibby has an energy and optimism that come from a deep appreciation of life as a gift, that doesn't go on for ever. Her *joie de vivre* is infectious and irrepressible. No wonder she is surrounded and adored by so many of the world's movers and shakers. She is also entirely pragmatic in appreciating how fortunate she is to be living in a part of the world where, for her, changing your life is an option. Faced with colon cancer at

60, she looked fear – and death – in the face and got on with living. It is this grasp of the preciousness of life that I believe fuels her perseverance and once her role as 'mummy' was over, propelled her out of an existence in the suburbs to an altogether less ordinary life.

Jibby's story testifies that with drive, determination and a little imagination, we can become something that we never thought possible before, at any age. She never gave up on life, or her dreams. And she reminds us that you can be a serious person without taking life too seriously, in spite of what you've endured. As she says, 'The show must go on!'

When Not to Persevere

Is there ever a time to cut your losses and run? Absolutely. When? That's up to you. Your call. Is there a difference between perseverance and stubbornness? Definitely. The best thing I can offer you is this: check your motivation. Why persist? What are you persevering for? Are you trying to sell something that no one wants, but you wish they would? Is your timing right? Are you too early with your big idea or too late? Is it unique enough, sufficiently outstanding? Have you lost interest? Are you persevering because 'giving up' makes you look bad? Do you *really* want what you say you want? Run a reality check and get to the bottom of what's going on and what you should do. Be decisive. Review the situation. Front up, tell the truth and decide to stay or go. Problems rarely get better on their own. Repeat, 'I approve of myself' and 'I trust myself' often and use these as your benchmarks. If you approved of yourself, what would you do and really want to do? These questions should form your line of inquiry.

At a talk I gave recently in London, one young man waited for over an hour in a queue to have his book signed and speak to me. His burning questions were: 'How can I strengthen my willpower? How can I make myself do things?' I simply pointed out that if he needed to summon so much willpower, did he really want the thing that much? He looked at me as if I'd just given him the secret to everlasting life! Like I say, check your motivation. If you're having to force yourself to do something so hard that it's an almighty struggle and no fun at all, maybe you just don't want it that much, any more? Above all – don't make your decision *personal*. Make it about the facts. Don't stick your head in the sand. Get on with making your decision and stand by it. Some years ago, Richard Branson closed down a magazine, *Event*, he'd just set up, *after two issues*. He simply said, 'The London market was saturated . . . it was a lost cause: *Time Out* was winning the circulation war, and I decided to cut our losses.' End of story. Nothing personal.

Then Again . . .

Sometimes, though, it really is better to keep going. But if perseverance isn't enough to get you through a difficult situation, and even optimism isn't working for you, you need hope. If you know that what you're doing is worth fighting for, you need to find some hope to bolster your perseverance. Hope is optimism's close cousin. Without hope, there are times and situations in life that would be impossible to endure. One man who has never given up hope in the thick of over thirty years of 'Troubles' in Northern Ireland is John Hume.

John is regarded as one of the most important figures in the history of Northern Ireland and the thinker behind many of the recent political developments that have led to the current peace process. He has served as an MP at Westminster and an MEP in Europe as well as a member of the Northern Ireland parliament. A former teacher, John Hume first came to prominence through the civil rights movement in the late 1960s, when Catholics demanded changes to the way Northern Ireland was run. In 1971, along with four other Northern Ireland MPs, he famously went on hunger strike close to 10 Downing Street to protest against internment. He helped found the moderate nationalist Social Democratic and Labour Party (SDLP) in 1970, taking over as its leader in 1979. Born in Derry in 1937, John was awarded the Nobel Peace Prize in 1998 for his efforts to find a peaceful solution to the conflict in Northern Ireland.

John Hume

My dream is that this generation will be the generation that takes the gun for ever off our streets and builds the new Ireland of the twenty-first century. The only way to get a solution among divided people is in victory, not in guns and bombs. As I have often said: We are a divided people, not a divided piece of earth. But to get an agreement obviously takes time and when you do finally reach that agreement, full implementation takes time as well. It requires a long healing process.

Bloody Sunday occurred on my own streets in Derry when British soldiers opened fire, killing thirteen innocent people and injuring fourteen others on the afternoon of Sunday 30 January, 1972. This incident particularly sticks in my mind. I didn't take part in that march because I had led one the week before on Magilligan Beach, where we'd been attacked, and I knew from the army's tactics that day that the march on the 30th would get the same treatment, probably worse. I had led a peaceful march to protest against internment and there were several thousand of us taking part. As we neared the internment camp we were stopped by members of the Green Jackets and the Parachute regiments. I remember the troops putting barbed wire around the beach to close it off. When it looked as if the marchers were going to go around the wire, the army then fired rubber bullets and CS gas straight at us. Many people were dragged off and badly beaten. There was just no way a civil rights march could have caused any trouble on a beach, so their response was completely unjustified. I knew then that trouble was brewing. I never guessed that it would turn out as badly as it did the next Sunday.

I feel we have a duty to create a society in which that never happens again. We are still awaiting the results of the public inquiry I campaigned for, all those years ago. A major objective is to make sure we never forget our past failures. The worst part is the loss of life and the number of human beings who have suffered. We should never forget the sacrifices the families made. The community as a whole has suffered for so long. But there is a completely different atmosphere on the streets now, compared to ten years ago, before the Good Friday peace agreement of 1998. I am now witnessing real progress. For the first time in history, the people have spoken on how they would like to live together in a truly democratic manner. The majority of the people have always been opposed to extremism, and violence, so I have always felt myself to be acting in the name of the majority.

When working to achieve lasting peace and a total end to violence, you have to keep hope alive. We need to give hope to our young people. The more they work together and break down the barriers of the past, the more they will realise that their common humanity transcends their differences. The healing process takes generations and there are difficulties but you have to keep your eye on the main road and stay on it.

I graduated in French and history and went on to do a Master's degree in history. I wrote about Derry in the nineteenth century. History has given me a sense of perspective and I appreciate how long major change and progress can take. History has shaped a lot of my thinking about Ireland and its future.

After university I went back to Derry and got involved in community politics. Myself and a local priest, Father Mulvey, set up the first housing association in Ireland. In the first year, we housed a hundred families. Then we put in major plans to build 700 houses and the local authority, which was Unionist-controlled, wouldn't give us planning permission. That led me straight into the civil rights movement, which led me directly into politics.

The 1960s was when the civil rights movement began in Northern Ireland and that was the period of Martin Luther King as well. He was an enormous influence. He was totally committed to non-violence. Even when you were being beaten on the streets, the message was: Don't retaliate. Let the world see who the real aggressor is. When I was growing up, the housing situation in the area was appalling. I don't know how the people stuck it – two to three families living in one house and the houses were so small. It was really terrible, but the civil rights movement achieved an awful lot. Unfortunately, the one area where we didn't make progress was on the jobs front. But one of the reasons for that was the start of the IRA campaign. To tackle the jobs problem, we needed investment, but the Troubles gave a bad image to the outside world. So the investment stopped.

I have found it hard at times to understand the violence and sectarianism in Northern Ireland. The people who are most sectarian would present themselves as the most religious and, being very Christian, I would simply want to remind them of the fundamental message of Christianity, which is 'Love thy neighbour'. I have never understood their sectarianism based on Christianity. There are three principles at the heart of our present peace agreement, which in my opinion will solve conflict anywhere in the world. Firstly – respect difference, acknowledging that difference is merely an accident of birth; secondly – create institutions that respect difference. The third principle is what I call the healing process, with people working together for their common interest, spilling sweat and not their blood. The real border in Ireland is in the minds and hearts of the people. Trust needs to replace the centuries of distrust and eventually the society that evolves will be one that respects difference.

I am very pleased that the whole of Europe is now united. Politics in the modern world is not about going to make speeches in Parliament. It's about making contacts on behalf of the people who elect you and serving the community as a whole. Real politics throughout Europe will be about the living standards of people, not about waving flags at one another. I hope we have left that behind in Ireland as well.

Meeting John Hume was for me like meeting a living legend. When I was a precocious and politicised ten-year-old growing up in Northern Ireland, he was one of my heroes, along with all the other leading figures of the time. My father was a founding member of the SDLP and my brother Brian was at Queen's University in Belfast along with many of the other youthful civil rights leaders. I joined them both on marches and felt deeply affected by what was going on around me. I remember exactly where I was and what I was doing on Bloody Sunday. Ten years later I left Northern Ireland, relieved to escape, having lived through the most violent years of the conflict. Brian had long since emigrated to Australia and my dad died shortly after I turned 20. I was keen to put Northern Ireland behind me, letting friends and all association with the place slip away. I came to London and softened my accent even further to avoid being identified and drawn into conversation about the Troubles. I had never understood how someone like John Hume could have stayed and persevered to bring about peace. How could he have kept hope alive? How could he see a better future?

I came away from our meeting in Westminster with greater understanding. Put simply: John is a visionary. He sees more than the immediate present; he sees way into the future. He also has a grasp of the past. It's no coincidence that he was deeply inspired by his 'absolutely brilliant history professor', Cardinal

O'Fiaich at Maynooth College. I suspect that in his bleakest times, he has felt history at his shoulder, insistently reminding him of past conflicts and resolutions, convincing him that change is possible. In his acceptance speech for the Nobel Peace prize, this is what he said:

> On my first visit to Strasbourg as a member of the European Parliament in 1979, I went for a walk across the bridge from Strasbourg to Kehl. Strasbourg is in France. Kehl is in Germany. They are very close. I stopped in the middle of the bridge and I meditated. There is Germany. There is France. If I had stood on this bridge thirty years ago after the end of the Second World War when 25 million people lay dead across our continent for the second time in history and if I had said, 'Don't worry, in thirty years' time we will all be together in a new Europe. Our conflicts and wars will be ended and we will be working together in our common interests,' I would have been sent to a psychiatrist. But it has happened . . . it is the duty of everyone, particularly those who live in areas of conflict, to study how it was done and to apply its principles to their own conflict resolution.

I suspect Hume's two great influences, Mahatma Gandhi and Martin Luther King, shared a similar hope and historical understanding.

The situation isn't always as dramatic as the Troubles in Northern Ireland or the conflict in Rwanda, which the subject of our next incredible case study lived through. Many of us have experienced periods of deep personal grief, or struggle, when a loved one has died or we ourselves have been ill. In truly difficult or distressing times, hope is the only thing that can fuel our perseverance. Even if the outcome is not wholly positive, there is always a better and a worse scenario, for ourselves and for others. Hope and perseverance can carry us through.

Sometimes a situation can be so urgent and extreme that you find almost superhuman strength to persevere and simply do what has to be done. Giving up just isn't an option because of the circumstances you find yourself in. Self-doubt doesn't feature because there is something far more demanding and critical to attend to. There is no room to waver. You do what you have to do because no one else will. As human beings, we never know how strong we really are until we're tested to the extreme, often in a war or life-and-death situation. Mary Kayitesi Blewitt has been tested in a way few of us will be. Read her story and you'll understand how, sometimes, perseverance is just pragmatic; the only option under the circumstances.

In April 1994, Hutus went on a killing spree against the minority Tutsis in Rwanda. Militia groups armed with machetes hacked their way through whole communities. In a hundred days, one million people were killed, more than 350,000 women raped (70 per cent of whom are now HIV positive) and many more maimed. Governments in the West did nothing until it was too late and, even now, few of those responsible have been brought to account.

Since the Rwandan genocide of 1994 claimed fifty of her relatives, including her 27-year-old brother, John Baptiste, who was killed in front of his wife and two young children, Mary Kayitesi Blewitt has devoted her life to helping survivors. She set up her charity, Survivors Fund (Surf, www.survivors-fund.org.uk) in 1997. Today, more than eleven years after the terrible massacre, 90 per cent of all work in Rwanda is supported solely by Survivors Fund and more than a thousand survivors live in London and depend on Mary. The 43-year-old was honoured for her work when she received the UK's Woman of the Year Award in 2005. She has lived in London since 1986 and is married to Richard, who works for the International Federation of the Red Cross (IFRC). They have a 14-year-old son and an 11-year-old daughter.

Mary Kayitesi Blewitt

Three weeks into the genocide, the militia came for my family. They were taken to the local school with the rest of the Tutsi families where they were attacked with machetes and thrown into a shallow pit. My 12-year-old niece crawled out and ran to a neighbour's house for help. They took her in, but the men raped her, over and over again. Eventually she was rescued by the Rwandan Patriotic Front. She is 24 now and still lives in Rwanda. She's a nurse, dedicating her life to looking after other survivors, but she will never marry.

A month after the genocide I went to Rwanda to look for the bodies of my family. The whole place still stank of death. There was a mass grave on the hillside but it wasn't deep enough. There was so much rain, it washed away the soil and there were bodies sticking out. But we couldn't bury them because there were still people searching desperately for their families. There were so many orphans – they were clinging on to me, begging me to take them. I spent eight months there working to reunite families.

When I came back to the UK, I couldn't forget about them. Initially my husband and I put down some personal finance to start the charity. Then when the Rwandan Embassy was just setting up, I worked there for about eight months. But it was too bureaucratic and huge and didn't offer the survivors enough so I left, with no job, no money coming in, and started my campaign from home with my husband supporting us both. I wrote to Oxfam who gave us £3,700 to buy a computer, which was our first big funding. Subsequently, other charities gave small sums to help with my travel, postage, etc. You don't realise how many overheads there are when you are starting out. I approached Trusts, Foundations, grant-award bodies, everyone, but was just hitting against a hard rock. I started attending conferences, asking people if they'd heard or done anything about the genocide. Then I decided that I couldn't spend my life trying to work out why it happened and why nobody cared. If I cared enough, I should do something about it. A few days ago I received £4.25 million from the British Government, but to date, there has simply been no time to obtain money and recognition because of the scale of the need of the widows and orphans. Of course, I was happy to be given the Woman of the Year award, but sad too. Had there been no genocide, I wouldn't need to do my job.

I have enough motivation for as long as I live because there is so much to do. I often feel helpless. There are a lot of expectations created by the fact that I have given my 100 per cent commitment to the survivors. I never get demoralised though. Some people only have me to turn to for help and support. If I don't deliver or use all of God's time, they will still be in the same position. Of course I get tired and don't have time for myself. I've lost the life I used to have but it is worth it when I receive cards and emails from the children addressing me as 'mother'. Their attachment is to me as a person, not to the charity. I've got about 10,000 children out there who think I'm their mother – which I think I am. If only I could put families back together, give these kids hope so they can give each other hope – that's where my helplessness lies.

I often think that if I had been in Rwanda at the time of the massacres, I'd have been a widow. I would definitely have been on a list of people to kill; I'd have spent a hundred days on the run or in hiding; I'd have been raped like all the women were and would probably be dying from HIV/Aids. I feel lucky that I escaped without pain and realise that I still have more of a life than they do. These people are in a situation where they cannot name a single family member, no matter how distant, and that is why I set up Survivors Fund.

The killing, the pain, the indifference are a long-term situation, yet the world wants to fix things quickly and get out. All the money raised in the UK was spent on setting up organisations in Rwanda to support survivors and helping a handful of survivors living in the UK. I struggle to this day to get these organisations to support the survivors.

Most charities don't work at the level of allowing the survivors to grow in their own time. The pain will never go away and the structures can't be rebuilt. Survivors Fund has been quietly listening to every single person. You end up with a whole lot of people who appear to be, but are not, mad. The pain translates into something you and I cannot ever understand.

I'm probably more aware of the daily situation in Rwanda than someone based in Kigali. I spend two to three months a year with the survivors; we build homes, dance all night and stay connected. I miss the motivation I get from them when I'm not there. We are so close – I can tell you what is happening to them at any moment.

When people ask me how I cope now, I think, this isn't about the last ten years; I've always coped and fought back. When I was growing up, there was poverty, fear, deaths you couldn't stop. My parents had to leave Rwanda during the 1959 revolution and settled in Uganda, though some of my family later returned. My father was a doctor and my mother a midwife. Most Rwandans couldn't get a job. When I was growing up, I didn't allow myself to be treated as a second-class citizen. My parents were always fighters. They always told us there was nothing we couldn't do. When my parents left Rwanda, half of my family were killed, so my parents had coped with a lot of trauma. They never talked about it.

I see myself as a human being and no different to any

other person. I have no hang-ups about personalities and respect people for who they are. I don't judge anyone or anything. I know personally, in my life, the things I've done have been due to the help of others. I now think: If it's really hard for me, how can it be easy for anyone else? I studied Political Science for my first degree and African Development Studies for my Master's but I can be anything – a president or a plumber. I do not have class or status in my head. As long as I am convinced that I am doing the right thing, I don't need to compare myself to anyone else. It doesn't matter to me about the awards we have won. I'm not berating people's attachment to these things. I am just a very simple person and can't make myself anything else. That's why I don't judge. I believe that giving people time is healthy. Not everything will work but you'll find something that you can comfortably achieve and be happy with. We should try to find a reason why we are here and build on it.

Ten years ago, the people I met in Rwanda didn't want to live. I try to give them hope. Now they have self-worth. I am the first one to know of their hope. When there is happy news, they want to share it with me. Many are starting to take control of their lives and time does heal. For me, being a Catholic has always played a very big part in my life. I sleep well and have peace of mind. I never brood – you have to solve matters and move on. If I had that extra burden to carry, I wouldn't be able to do the work I do.

I strongly believe that hard work is vital. We can't be good at everything but we need to keep trying to find out what it is that we are good at. You have to have humanity, appreciate people around you and respect everyone. The genocide might be the most horrific inspiration, but it forced me to discover I have the strength I have. Is that a good or a bad thing? I don't know.

* * *

I have rarely met a more down-to-earth and level-headed person than Mary, yet she is surrounded by a type of horror and suffering that most of us will never know. Sitting in the tiny Surf office in Fulham, I found it difficult to listen to her talk and admit I broke down halfway through our meeting, overwhelmed by the sheer, unbelievable awfulness of the whole situation. Interestingly, Mary simply allowed me time to compose myself before continuing. She wasn't unsympathetic but it occurred to me that she must have borne witness to other people's distress so many times before that it's something she is totally at ease with.

Perseverance is not something Mary has ever really thought about. She did what she had to do after the genocide because there was no one else to do it. Seeing the difference her work makes to people's lives fuels her to continue. Witnessing the resilience of the human spirit in people who have lost everything and, sometimes, everyone, clearly keeps her hope alive. Undoubtedly, her strong Catholic faith gives her tremendous sustenance as well.

I found it remarkable that Mary is such a peaceful and cheerful person. I felt relaxed and at ease with her the instant we met and others have made the same observation. She has a presence that I can only describe as serene and light and very calming to be around. Perhaps this is the result of a lifetime of struggle, refusing to be diminished, let alone destroyed by it. 'Anger is so self-destructive but hate is even worse because that kills you,' she says. 'There has to be something positive to come out of all this bad.'

When Mary suggested I join her on her next trip to Rwanda, I laughed and said I didn't think I'd be much use, given my earlier feebleness. She said I'd actually be fine, because I'd see people just getting on with everyday life, doing what has to be done and making the best of everything, and I'd join in and do the same. I suppose that's just it: in extreme situations you just get on and do what has to be done. Perseverance becomes automatic.

The strongest message to take away from the example of all the people in this chapter is that perseverance is easier when you have a worthwhile cause, one you believe is worth fighting for. Michelle Mone stiffened her resolve to stand up to her opponents because she knew she was right and deserved to win; Jibby was striving for a more meaningful and authentic life and to help young artists; John Hume may have grown despondent at times but he never doubted the importance of his work; while Mary knew that she could not walk away from the suffering she had witnessed. The second outstanding feature of these individuals is their attitude of hope and optimism. Mary's outlook is all the more striking because of the harrowing circumstances; she never despaired of human beings even though she had seen them at their worst. Instead she allowed her hope to be fuelled by the strength and optimism she saw in people who had lost everything but still wanted to rebuild their lives.

While we might marvel at the spirit and tenacity of all these individuals, it is worth bearing in mind that we may only know our own strength when we are ourselves tested. Starting out as a naïve young girl, Michelle had no idea of the cut-throat world she would have to deal with in the lingerie trade and became well-nigh invincible in the process. While Mary wishes that her work was not necessary, she acknowledges that it has transformed her.

In other words, you don't know the measure of your own mettle until you are called upon to use it. Whatever the challenge, don't assume that it would be beyond you. Instead, grasp that you are stronger than you think and know that you'll generate the wherewithal to handle whatever life throws at you. Perseverance can show you what you're made of.

Five Steps to Greater Perseverance

1. What are you persevering for? It's a lot easier and more fun to persist and push for what you *really* want rather than what you – or other people – think you should want. If things aren't working out, check for self-sabotage. It could be one way of covertly saving yourself. Know the difference between effort and struggle.

2. Get back on track. When you mess up, get back on track quickly. Revel in your mistake until you're clear why you made it, then pick yourself up and start again with a clean slate.

3. Be real. Be optimistic. Awful things can happen at any moment, so you may as well be pleased while they are not. Seriously. And remember that optimism is good for you. It will keep you going through difficulty and for the rest of your life. Success can come at any age so long as you keep believing that and working for it.

4. Lean on others. Each of the great perseverers in this chapter had a great person behind them, building them up, lending vital strength when theirs was running low. A supportive partner is a tremendous bonus. If they're not in your life right now, take strength from pals, comrades and colleagues.

5. Don't defeat yourself. Watch your self-fulfilling prophecies. Don't set yourself up to fail, before or during your endeavours. Your abilities are at the mercy of your beliefs. Neither are fixed. Don't let yourself down!

7: *Be* GENEROUS

You may wonder what generosity has to do with success, or making money, or happiness. Business manuals and success guides of old have tended to focus purely on the attainment of material goals as the measure of our success and satisfaction with life. But times change. Today, we're much more aware of alternative ways to measure success and increasing numbers of us regard our time and fulfilment as more precious than a huge salary. In the developed world we've never been healthier or wealthier.

Happiness and Success

Gandhi put it well when he said, 'Happiness is when what you think, what you say, and what you do are in harmony.' Nowadays that works as a pretty good definition of how we're coming to see success. My observation and conversations with happy, successful achievers has shown me that living and working with a generous approach to life pays big dividends. On a personal level, being generous leaves you feeling better about yourself, giving you that elusive feeling of fulfilment and satisfaction that we know money can't buy.

In business, generosity brings you career advancement and opportunities that meaner 'jobsworth' individuals envy and don't understand. And if you're running the business, quite simply, people will want to work for you and stay with you.

On 24 August 2001 People Management reported on research concerning the career aspirations of 14-year-olds. Stephen Gauntlet, one of the report's authors, said, 'The most important factor when considering a career was that it be "a job that interests me" followed by "pay" and then "time for interests outside work".' He also commented: 'Five to ten years ago, people were looking for power. Now they are looking for fulfilment.'

I usually coach people further down the line, when the factors in choosing a company to work for, or stay with, have been narrowed down to one word, 'culture'. At a certain senior level, the 'packages' all look pretty similar. What makes the difference are things like, what the company stands for, its vision, its ethics, its social responsibility, how it treats its staff – and not just at the top.

Happiness and Generosity

Studies consistently indicate that voluntary work benefits the person doing it as much as the person receiving it. It elevates one's own happiness, physical health, self-respect and sense of being able to make a difference in own one's life as well as to someone else's.

In 2005, which was designated the Year of the Volunteer, a nationwide campaign coaxed us all to help others. An ICM poll at the time showed that a quarter of volunteers believed it helped them lose weight, 61 per cent say it helped them feel less stressed, and a surprising 15 per cent reported eating less chocolate!

Another study, at the University of California at Riverside, also showed how we can influence our levels of happiness through practical means. Carrying out five acts of kindness a week brought the testers a 'significantly increased satisfaction' with life, compared with those who didn't. The acts of kindness were both random and regular, such as helping a struggling parent with their pram upstairs or making a meal for an elderly neighbour once a week. Sonja Lyubomirsky, a psychologist at the university, says: 'They make you feel generous and capable and give you a greater sense of connection with others.'

Random Acts of Kindness is the title of a book with a worldwide cult following, selling purely by word of mouth. It was published in 2003 by Danny Wallace, a 29-year-old journalist and comedy writer. The book lists 365 'ways to make the world a nicer place'. You may also have seen 'Join Me' posters in cities all over the world, with a website address, Join-Me.co.uk. urging you to join the author's karma army or cult of kindness. The cult has a simple message: *Undertake a random act of kindness for a stranger when you can.*

My favourite example in Danny's book was provided by Lorna Mann in Sydney: 'I met a bloke called Jeff the other night whose life has changed thanks to a random act of kindness. He was a rich restaurateur who was sitting on a park bench one night when a homeless fella walked up and offered him his only possession: his blanket. The homeless guy thought Jeff must be homeless too . . . And yet was willing to give away the only thing he owned. It had such an impact on Jeff that he packed in his restaurant and started a non-religious charity that now feeds 500 people a night . . . That was ten years ago. And what happened to the original homeless guy? He was best man at Jeff's wedding!'

I love this book – and the cult – because it makes kindness cool and fun, rather than the preserve of pious and pompous do-gooders. The postings on the website are predominantly from twenty- and thirtysomethings, the supposedly 'me' generation, traditionally consumed with career success, getting ahead and out-and-out hedonism. But the Random Acts of Kindness cult has struck a chord with young people everywhere. Clearly, once people get a taste for this type of satisfaction, they like it and want more.

Spurred on by Danny's book, I looked for an opportunity to carry out my own Random Act of Kindness and see how it felt. Here's what I did. That evening I went to my local gastro-pub where my son Jamie and I had become regulars, as the food was truly sensational. We noticed how all the thanks and tips went to the waiting staff, but never to the chef, who was the one responsible for the fabulous fare. Although we had never actually seen him, we had heard him – expressing himself very clearly in the kitchen on a few occasions! We decided to write a compliment note to him, thanking him for his wonderful, best-ever cooking and promising to spread the word. The note was dispatched to the kitchen with our waitress.

Seconds later, a sweaty young man emerged from the kitchen. Neil was so shocked by our note that he had come in search of his secret admirers. He explained that no one had ever taken the trouble to thank him before (including the pub's owner) and he was really touched. At only 24, Neil was pushing himself six nights a week to turn out some of the best food I'd ever seen or tasted. He was passionate about what he did and we were the first diners to acknowledge this. Jamie and I went home feeling ecstatic, our happiness levels soaring off the scale!

A few months later, when I mentioned to Neil that my birthday was approaching and I'd be bringing about eight friends over to eat, he said he'd like to give me a present. He wanted to be my personal chef for the evening, come to my flat and cook a birthday meal in my own kitchen! The only money he would consider taking was the cost of the food and wine, which would all be at trade price. Neil discussed menus with me and then took care of everything, buying the food, cooking it, and clearing up afterwards. He even brought his girlfriend to waitress! It was a wonderful evening and everyone raved about Neil's food, particularly one of my guests who also happened to be a restaurant critic. Neil left the pub not long after that to become a shareholder and run the kitchen in a swanky new bar and restaurant and I had acquired the taste for regular and Random Acts of Kindness!

I'm in good company too. While the world's greatest rock star, Bono, is well known for his worldwide altruism, the world's greatest film star, Brad Pitt, has just joined the Make Poverty History campaign to end world poverty, has already spent time in Africa and is planning regular trips to do what he can. Here's someone who can afford to be entirely wrapped up in his own superstar world, protected from other's problems, and yet feels a human need to expand his horizons to be generous to others. When you've got everything the world has to offer, perhaps you have to be inventive about further sources of happiness and fulfilment.

Generosity in Business

Running a business that displays generosity towards its staff, the environment, the bigger picture, is one that customers find attractive. Big and small businesses are being forced to get ethical and fair as never before. Putting profit before everything else is just not something that any business can really afford to do any more. We saw this with the boycott of Barclays Bank way back in the 1960s and '70s, when customers left in their thousands to protest against what they saw as the bank's involvement in the apartheid state of South Africa. Nowadays, the Co-operative Bank, motto 'Customer-led, ethically guided', is enjoying greater success than ever before as it proclaims its ethical investment policy, promising not to use customers' money to invest in the arms industry or the tobacco industry, or to accept customers from those industries. Boycotts of brands and mayday protests have created headlines.

Barely a week goes by without an undercover documentary highlighting where our high-street chains get their clothes made, urging us shoppers to check with our local Gap and Nike supplier to ensure they're not employing 12-year-olds in their factories in the Far East. A recent *Panorama* documentary exposed the horrendous working conditions which produce 'dollar-a-day dresses'. As I write this, the *Independent* newspaper has published a shoppers' guide to garden furniture, naming and shaming the garden centres and DIY stores that use wood from the Brazilian rainforests. There's even a new chain of coffee shops on our streets offering only fair-trade coffee, and Tayto crisps that I grew up with in Ireland have just launched a new range called 'honest' crisps! And Fairtrade, the foundation that promotes coffee, chocolate and bananas produced by farmers' co-operatives that receive a fair price for their products, has just announced a 50 per cent rise in sales.

Consumer pressure is a big deal. A report in March 2005 by Mintel, the consumer analyst, said that well-informed customers were 'taking a more individual and personal approach to the choices they make and are rebelling against mass marketing'. We want to enjoy our goods without it ruining our health, depleting the earth or exploiting people in other parts of the world. Generosity in business today is an absolute must.

As a dedicated follower of fashion, I keep up with the trends. And one that is about to be everywhere is 'ethical chic'. Fashion writers predict that it will be all the rage, enabling people to 'look good while doing good'. In June 2005 the Fairtrade Foundation launched its fashion 'mark' – a clothes label that gives shoppers a guarantee that cotton farmers in West Africa and India get a better deal. The charity is in talks with leading high-street chains and it's confident that many of the big stores will be selling ethically-produced clothes in the next few years. 'The public is hungry for these products. Shops just cannot keep up with demand for fair trade,' says Harriet Lamb, the foundation's executive director. She adds, 'One person's bargain is another person's tragedy and farmers often end up getting very, very low prices for their produce. There is a move against that by the public.'

Intriguingly, the current issue of the fashion bible *Vogue* and just about every other one of the glossies and weekend supplements have featured the launch of a new label, Edun. Bono and his wife, Ali Hewson, have teamed up with hip American designer Rogan Gregory (he of the hottest jeans around) to create a 'socially conscious apparel brand'. Edun will have no Asian sweatshops employing underpaid children to churn out garments made from chemically treated materials. From cotton field to factory to shop to customer – the founding principle behind the label is that everyone in the chain benefits. In the words of Bono, 'It's conscious consumerism. Shopping is becoming a political act. People are seeing that with their dollar or their pound, they can change a lot. They can close down giant petroleum companies just by not putting that company's petrol in their tank. They can close down food companies by not buying their food.' Will the label take off and, with it, the idea of a brand with conscience? Given that U2 will be wearing and selling Edun clothes during their world tour and they are in talks with other bands, including Coldplay and REM, to do likewise, it's looking good. And the clothes are very cool too. Ali Hewson points out, 'We're not selling hairshirts. We want people to feel that there's a choice in the market for them, to buy and wear clothes that look good – and that they can feel good about.' Given the thumbs-up from *Vogue*, stocked by Selfridges in London, Saks in New York, Brown Thomas in Ireland and selected other stores, I'd say they're off to a good start.

Innocent Drinks epitomises the new breed of ethical business. They treat their customers like friends, welcoming correspondence and replying by sending back the Innocent rulebook, the company's light-hearted manifesto about living a healthier life, giving lots of money to charity and selling only the best juices. Innocent treat their staff well too. There is an annual snow-boarding holiday and a £2,000 cash gift to every baby born to an Innocent staffer. On Friday evenings, the company encourages staff to leave early by putting a couple of hundred pounds behind the bar at the local. Innocent gives a high proportion of its profits to charity and is also one of Britain's most successful companies. Their drinks are available at Tesco, Sainsbury's, Waitrose, Selfridges and Starbucks (among other places) and last year's turnover was £15 million.

Adam Balon, Richard Reed and Jon Wright, all 32, met at college and launched Innocent in 1999. The UK smoothie market is worth £70 million a year and in just over five years, Innocent has taken more than 30 per cent of the market share.

Adam Balon

We always talked about running a business together at college and we never really let go of that dream. So we asked ourselves: 'What is it that annoys us about life and what could we do to make it easier or better?' Pretty utopian, pretty simple, but actually quite a persuasive way of thinking about it. The conversation happened during the course of a long car journey together. We had fifteen hours to kill so we discussed those things that really get to us and we all agreed that what we really wanted, and that was missing from the market, was something that would do us good, something healthy. We all went out a lot, worked hard, lived a typical urban lifestyle, and we realised it was actually pretty difficult to do anything that was really good for you. For example, it was much easier to eat a kebab on the way home after a night out than it was to get some fresh stuff in you. Then we figured that there had to be other people who felt the same way. We did come up with a few other ideas but the fruit juice was the one that survived the car journey and subsequent holiday, and we thought: Actually, you know, this sounds really good, we could really do this. So we then decided to get a business plan together.

We were still working in our full-time jobs at the time so Innocent Drinks, born from that car journey in 1998, didn't actually come about until the spring of 1999. At that point we were working on it in our spare time. The first thing we did was some research. I'd go out and talk to shopkeepers to try to find out a little bit about what they wanted from their products and then we started contacting fruit suppliers. By the summer of '98 we had even worked out how to make smoothies and bored our friends rigid with questionnaires, so we used the Parsons Green jazz festival to try the whole thing out. We bought £500 worth of fruit, made it into smoothies, put them on a stall with a huge sign which read, 'Shall we give up our day jobs?' and encouraged people to vote with their empty cups, placing them in 'yes' bins and 'no' bins. By the end of the event the 'yes' bin was full and the 'no' bin was pretty much empty.

We all resigned from our jobs the next day. It was August and we expected to be on the market by September. Of course things took a hell of a lot longer than we thought. So that was a fairly bleak time for us – we lived off credit cards. We didn't go out and we basically survived on cornflakes and soup! It was fine at first and all very exciting but after six months of living like this we were thinking, My God, when are we ever going to launch this? We were struggling to raise money but when we went to see the banks they just weren't interested. What they saw were these three enthusiastic guys with no experience in the area. We weren't a very good investment prospect.

So in the end we just sent an email around to absolutely everybody we knew, asking, 'Do you know anyone rich?' And amazingly, we got a reply from someone who Jon used to work with, saying he had worked with some guy called Maurice Pinto, a 65-year-old investor who invested in ongoing companies rather than start-ups like us. We decided it was worth sending him a business plan anyway, and we went for a meeting. In the end, Maurice ended up backing the entire venture and although we didn't make any profit until the third year, that's pretty much what we expected. And since then, it's gone beyond anything we could have imagined.

The thing about the business for us isn't about profit maximisation in the short term. We need a business that can be profitable but for us it's more about growing a decent sustainable business we can be proud of. And that pride applies to everything we do. We want to make the kind of smoothies you would make at home. I put our success down to the fact that that we are still the only company to offer 100 per cent fresh fruit in a bottle; though not all the fruit is organic, it's as near as; and we are totally pesticide-free. All the other bottled brands use sugar and water to bulk up their drinks or fruit concentrates. It costs more to do it our way, but our customers are discerning. We spent a year trying to find someone who could make smoothies to the standard we wanted. The food industry thought we were mad; you don't use strawberries, you use this great strawberry flavouring. I hate seeing something run as a business, not a passion. We are ruthlessly nice. We employ people like us – people who would never work for a tobacco company – and that just keeps working in our favour.

We didn't pay back Maurice as he took a stake in the business, so he is in fact still involved. In 2004 Innocent Drinks had a turnover of £15 million, which is a far cry from eating cornflakes and living off credit cards. It's been absolutely brilliant, and whatever happens we're still a small business and we've all enjoyed the journey. All three of us have this pathological fear of being average, so for us now it's all about attention to detail.

> *We want more than anything to be Europe's favourite little juice company. We're always thinking, What can we do to improve things? We drive around in 'cow' vans and we've got grass on the floor in the office. We don't want to be the biggest: we want to be the best. We met some people from Unilever the other day. They were interested in how we do business. We said, 'Be natural. Be nice.' They went on, earnestly, 'That sounds great. Now how do you implement that strategy of being nice?' We replied, 'We want to connect with the people who drink our products. Our products are totally fresh and natural, and we think they taste gorgeous!'*

Innocent drinks really are the best! They stand out a mile from the competition and the personality of the company comes through as well. I love the humour that lists '10 pebbles' as one of the ingredients, explaining at the bottom, 'Only joking!' I love the taste and quality. I love that Innocent are nice and fair to their staff. And I really love that they plough a lot of the profit back into supporting the replanting of trees in Brazil. Here's what they say on the pineapple, banana and coconut cartons, under the heading, 'It's nice to be nice': 'It's all very well making tasty drinks, but it's quite nice to be able to help people out as well. That's why we've formalised our commitment to being truly innocent by setting up the Innocent Foundation. It's a separate registered charity that funds non-governmental organisations in the countries where we source our fruit. And the funding of the charity is directly linked to how many drinks we sell, so the more you drink, the more you help.' Below this is a photo of a Brazilian rainforest, with a plot circled, to show where your money is going.

When you get all this with your smoothie, why would you ever dream of buying an 'ordinary' one ever again? That would be no fun at all.

Generosity and Making Money

It's obvious that a company that treats its staff well will have their loyalty and keep them for longer. But treating your staff well also benefits the bottom line, as happy staff tend to feel a high level of respect and honesty towards their company. Put simply, happy staff don't steal from the business, whereas disrespect and meanness breed resentment. And resentment often seeks redress, however irrational. Here's an example. A young friend, Rory, has just finished his pilot training and is about to start his first job with BA (British Airways). He is full of inside information about the airline industry and how pilots feel about the various airlines. One immensely profitable low-cost airline is shunned by pilots due to their appallingly mean-spirited treatment by the management. Pilots are pushed to fly the absolute maximum hours permitted, and have to pay for their own uniforms and airport car-parking expenses. They even have to buy their own drinking water from the drinks trolley during flights! What the management may not realise is that this shoddy treatment of their staff is costing them vast amounts of money every day. Instead of flying at the most fuel-efficient altitude and speeds, pilots will deliberately fly at a less efficient altitude and speed. On a typical two-hour flight, this can waste as much as half a ton of fuel, costing around £400 at the current market price. Over the course of a week a pilot could fly this journey up to sixteen times, costing the company in the region of £6,000. And that's just one pilot on one aircraft.

Interestingly, the original US low-cost airline that inspires all the others, Southwest Airlines, is one of the most loved by pilots. They treat their staff with great respect and pilots rarely leave. Senior pilots that Rory has spoken to have said that they would take a job there even if it meant a drop in salary or seniority, simply because it is such a great company to work for. Southwest Airlines is an immensely profitable company that has never had to make anyone redundant for cost-cutting reasons. It really does pay to be generous.

Everyday Generosity

Being a generous consumer as well as employer is one of the simplest but most powerful things you can do. But there are lots of others. Take time to make a list of generosity ideas, whereby you can channel generosity into your life and the lives of those around you. I believe that building generosity into your character makes you a bigger, more expansive individual, more interesting, more compelling to be with. People respond to generosity as though it feeds their soul and reminds them of how great the human spirit can be. And they pay back that generosity many times over. I write this sitting at a secluded, sought-after table at my local Italian restaurant where I never have to think about booking. Why do I get this VIP treatment? Simply because I gave away a basket that Sylvia, the *maître d'*, fell in love with. I could see that it would be perfect for her to take on holiday the very next day, so I emptied out my belongings and gave it to her. This apparently grand, but incredibly easy, gesture on my part overwhelmed her. Her response was thanks enough for me but I can't deny that my star treatment isn't incredibly pleasant. If you think this sounds pious, think again. I liked the bag – she loved it. I could see the pleasure she would get from it. And that made my evening in itself. Don't take my word for it. Just try it. It's a wonderful feeling.

Being generous doesn't have to stop at material things. Every day we are presented with opportunities to extend generosity to another person and leave them feeling better about themselves. Over seventy years ago, Dale Carnegie wrote in his million-selling success manual, *How to Win Friends and Influence People*: 'Try honestly to make the other person feel important, and do it sincerely.' His message is as true today as it was then. His book can be summed up in the following instructions:

1. The other person is important. You have little to gain by undermining them. Become genuinely interested in other people.

2. At work your relationship with employers and co-workers is vital to get the work done well.

3. People are much more than their job description implies. Give each person's life sincere consideration, taking into account their personal story and challenges.

4. Learn from experiences of others that which you could not know simply from the experiences you have had yourself.

5. Be a good listener. Encourage others to talk about themselves. Talk in terms of the other person's interests. Smile.

Being generous doesn't take anything away from you but it benefits everyone. When a friendship needs mending, when someone has to make the first move, be big enough to be that person. Pick up the phone and make contact. Everyday interactions with people in shops or in service call centres give us ample opportunity to extend respect to people who may get ignored or verbally abused. Another obvious opportunity to offer generosity is simply to listen – *really* listen – to older people, at a bus stop, with a neighbour, in a supermarket queue. You'll make their day and it need take only a few minutes out of yours.

Be Generous to Yourself

It's easier to feel generous to others when you're generous to yourself. It's hard to give something away that you don't already have. Being mean to yourself while you are generous to others will leave you feeling resentful and empty. Are you generous to a fault – the fault being that you neglect yourself? How generous are you to you? Here's a simple questionnaire to get you thinking. Tick the answer that best describes your situation.

1. I feel put upon by other people's demands:
   a) all the time, and find it impossible to say no; b) quite often, with so much of my time taken up attending to others; c) rarely, and I enjoy those times when I do help someone else out; d) never. I have very clear boundaries and it takes all my time and energy just to sort my own life out.

2. I feel exhausted and utterly drained:
   a) all the time, and often feel I'm on the verge of getting ill; b) quite often, and I certainly have no spare energy for taking exercise or going to the gym; c) rarely, and when I do it's after a tough gym workout or an unusually long day at work; d) never. I always preserve my own energy, otherwise my life simply would not work.

3. I feel resentful towards others, including close friends and family:
   a) all the time. I seem to exist to make everyone else's lives work; b) quite often, but I can't see any other way if people need me; c) rarely. Sometimes I say yes when I should have said no, but it's not a problem; d) never. I don't allow others to overstep the mark.

4. I bottle things up and avoid confrontation or sometimes just explode:
   a) all the time. I don't know how it could be any different; b) quite often, and I do find it very upsetting; c) rarely. I prefer not to sit on a problem, but to get it sorted ASAP; d) never. I pride myself on being straight with people even if it makes me unpopular.

5. I feel that good luck and great things happen to other people and not me:
   a) all the time. I'm just not a lucky person, and it feels like it's a dog-eat-dog world; b) quite often. Life takes hard work. Nothing has ever been given free to me; c) rarely. What goes around comes around. I get my fair share of luck and opportunities; d) never. I don't sit around waiting for things to come to me. If I want something, I go out and get it.

How Did You Score?

Mostly a's: You're generous to a fault and on the road to total burn-out. Stop being such a martyr and begin to take care of yourself. You are showing no kindness or generosity to yourself and must be seething with resentment as you give, give, give. Pull back immediately and rethink how you're living. It's vital for your overall health and happiness that you value yourself more highly. Imagine what your life would be like if you prioritised your own needs and wants in the way that you do other people's.

Mostly b's: There's not a lot of generosity going on here for you. Before you say yes to another request, stop and think: Am I being generous to myself here? Can I really do this or will it take up all my energy and free time? If I was to be generous to myself, what would I do? Repeat to yourself: I deserve to take care of myself. I approve of myself. I like myself.

You need to get better at receiving as opposed to giving. Being generous to yourself includes accepting generosity from others. Allow other people to give to you in the measure that you give to them.

Mostly c's: You've got a good balance here of taking care of yourself and caring for other people. Sometimes it's worth saying yes to others when we'd rather say no because it means so much to them and our personal inconvenience is outweighed by their appreciation. You understand this. Stay vigilant to your decisions and ensure that you maintain that overall healthy balance.

Mostly d's: No one's going to get the better of you! But be careful that your rigid boundaries don't imprison you, leaving you isolated and cut off. Life seems such a battle for you. You appear overly defensive and mean in your approach. Your lot could be easier with more co-operation and less competition. And you'd feel less of a need to guard yourself and keep others at a distance. Take a risk and try being more trusting and generous with people. You could enjoy the feeling. If you get let down, resist temptation to revert to form and keep on staying open to being generous. Don't neglect to notice what you're getting back in return.

But how does being generous help you get ahead in your career? How does it help you stand out, be noticed, get on the board and become a significant shareholder, especially when you left school with no qualifications? Chris Sade began his working life washing dishes at 16 and ended up at 29 as the president of the US arm of the company, a board director and a major shareholder in the overall group. He now runs the private members' club and hotel, Soho House in New York, has just opened another in LA and has plans to open clubs in Miami, Las Vegas, San Francisco and the Hamptons. Chris arrived in London from Belgium with just £500 in savings. You'll recognise some of the references from Rule 4: **Take More Risks**, where you met Chris's boss, Nick Jones!

Chris Sade

When I moved to London I really didn't speak much English, well, I didn't speak English at all! My dad's from Morocco, my mum's from Belgium. I left Morocco at the age of ten, where I was living with my dad, and moved to Belgium to be with my mum. We lived in a small town about 25 kilometres from Brussels, which for a teenager was pretty boring. I came to London because I thought London was probably a lot more exciting.

As it didn't require me to do much talking I took a job washing dishes at a place called Over The Top in Fulham. One day Nick (Jones) walked into the kitchen and found me cooking my own lunch. He seemed surprised that I could cook and since we needed chefs, he asked me if I was interested. Actually, I had pretty much no experience of cooking but three months later the head chef left and Nick asked me to take over. It was quite tough. At first I had to rely on the waitresses to draw pictures of the order! But I started picking up the language and soon I felt I'd got the hang of the kitchen. Before long I started to think about leaving and going travelling. Nick sat me down and said, 'Look, I think you should stay. I think you've got potential to be one of the managers,' and I laughed. I remember thinking he was mad. Then I thought, What have I got to lose? I'll stick around. I spent six months running the bar and then I moved on to become manager. I was about 20.

But Over The Top was going downhill very fast and Nick had to do something drastic. He went to Paris to see what really worked there, and came back with the idea for Café Bohème. Those were tough times but I just kept working, running the bar. I literally worked all hours. I did nothing but work and obviously that was noticed. My shift would usually start at five in the evening but I'd come in at twelve o'clock and help out with whatever I could. Then normally everyone would leave at two in the morning and I'd still be there at four o'clock making sure everything was fine. There was a part of me trying to prove to someone that I could do well – or perhaps to myself. I think it was probably due to the way I was brought up, in a broken family, with my thinking I was never really gonna make it. I hung on to the belief that I could achieve what I wanted to achieve, but I knew it wasn't going to happen just like that: I wasn't going to land on my feet without any effort. I accepted that I'd have to work very hard for it and I was prepared to do whatever it took to get there.

I spent two years working round the clock to make Café Bohème a success, which was a huge relief after all the uncertainty, then Nick came up with the idea of Soho House. I remember saying to him, 'Do it! This is a fantastic idea, it's going to do well. It's unique, we're going to create something fantastic.' And we did. When it opened, Nick told me he was going to hand over complete responsibility for Café Bohème to me. It was quite overwhelming. I remember the day we sat in with the board and one of the board members expressed concern that I was not sufficiently experienced, that sales would fall. I would have felt exactly the same in his position but I remembered Nick saying, 'I've got complete belief that Chris will do a great job and probably do it even better than me.' Then I felt this huge pressure not just keep to it as it is, but to try to make it even better.

I went in there with that attitude and with a bit of luck and a lot of hard work the sales increased and everyone started making money. I wanted to make it a great place people would love to come to. I believed in it and I was determined to keep aiming higher. It was someone else's but I treated it much as if it were my own. I probably wouldn't have worked as hard if it had been mine. In fact, I definitely wouldn't have worked that hard if it had been mine! The first year there was probably a 20 per cent increase in sales and then each year it grew even better than the year before. To achieve that was quite remarkable for such a small place. I felt this huge loyalty and gratitude to Nick for believing in me and giving me a chance to prove myself.

A couple of years after we opened Soho House we started to feel very confident about it and I still wanted to do more, to do different things. Nick came up with the idea of Babington House and despite the industry's scepticism, again, I felt inspired. I felt excited.

So we went ahead and opened Babington House and I went down to Somerset and actually lived there for a year. I lived in a little cottage which is up at the top of the drive. That's when Nick formally brought me into the business as a shareholder. After Babington was up and running and clearly a success, the next step was New York! As Nick had a wife and family and I was single, it was obvious that I should be the one to move to New York and set things up there. It was a nightmare getting the place ready to open – New York builders are every bit as difficult as British ones! But it's working. Here I am, a shareholder in the overall business, president of Soho House Inc. in the US. We've just opened in LA. After that, maybe Miami, maybe San Francisco, maybe the Hamptons. I have a significant stake in the entire Soho House business.

I've been given great chances and breaks. As someone who arrived in London at 16, not speaking the language, with no qualifications, I'm happy!

* * *

Can't you just see how invaluable Chris made himself to Nick? I commented to Nick, when I interviewed him, that he had been so lucky to have Chris by his side and he agreed, admitting that he had often spent more time with him than with his wife! From the start, Chris's attitude was one of total personal responsibility and doing a great job, way beyond just working his shift. He treated the business as his own and ended up being Nick's right-hand man by supporting and backing every bright idea and new business venture, when most others were urging caution.

Don't make the mistake of thinking Chris was some martyr. He had his own agenda and ambitions and I guess that if he hadn't been offered breaks and opportunities in return for his contribution, he would have gone to find them elsewhere. Witness his search for a new challenge after the success of their country house hotel, Babington House. That's what gave birth to the US arm of the business. So, there's an important lesson here – value your generosity. If it's not being repaid by generosity, think about taking it elsewhere. Remember Neil, the brilliant, unappreciated chef? The gastro-pub went into receivership within six months of his departure but his new place is thriving round the corner. If you're lucky enough to have a Chris or a Neil around you, hang on to them by being generous with their dreams and aspirations.

When I met up with Chris in New York in December 2003, I laughed that being with Soho House was the only job he had actually ever had! He agreed. 'But there was never any need for me to leave. Any time I felt bored or I wanted to do something different, Nick was right there with an idea or promotion and I always felt so darned grateful to him for trusting in my potential and letting me prove myself time and time again.'

Mind you, it's not that hard to warm to a generous person. As I was leaving, Chris insisted I come back that evening and sample the restaurant, compliments of the house. Furthermore, their New Year's Eve party, the very next evening, which was the talk of New York, would be fabulous and I shouldn't miss that either and he'd put me on the guest list immediately. See what I mean?

What's the difference between running a successful profit-orientated business and one where you have a direct impact on people's lives? How does it feel to move from pure profit-and-loss to helping people improve their lives? Former Northern Ireland Businesswoman of the Year, Pamela Morgan, knows. She has enjoyed fabulous success with her family business, having taken it over from her father twenty-five years ago as a young graduate, to run with her two brothers. The annual turnover at Component Distribution Ltd was then £500,000 and is now in excess of £15 million.

Pamela Morgan

I started working for the family business straight out of university at 21 and by the time I was 27, I had become Operational Director. We distribute vehicle parts to over two hundred garages and bodyshops throughout Ireland. Dad said in the early days he thought I'd do it for a few years then go off and start a family. I come from a traditional, patriarchal background. Ironically, I was probably the most driven out of his three children. I felt a terrific need to prove myself and be successful. I pushed the business into different areas, moved it into the south of Ireland, expanded what we offered and set up the training school.

I have had to be truly immersed in this business for it to be a success. I've spent twenty years in the car industry and I'm passionate about it. There was never enough time for a husband and two children because I was completely focused on it. I enjoyed it. I really wanted to build it up and move it on another step.

I got the idea of setting up a training school for mechanics about ten years ago. I noticed that there was an incredible shortage of skilled mechanics, especially crash repair experts, and not enough quality training. Initially, I wasn't getting anywhere with my plan because people didn't believe you could have apprenticeship training within the private sector. So I wrote to Mo Mowlam, the then Secretary of State for Northern Ireland. She got in touch immediately and was incredibly enthusiastic and supportive. She set up a meeting with the head of what is now the Department of Education and Skills. He agreed to give me a pilot scheme to run with fourteen apprentices and in 1998, we opened our school, Blackwater House, Centre for Career Development, just outside Belfast. We now have over two hundred apprentices.

I would go into schools to try to market the motor trade as a valid career. The kids all wanted to go into more sexy industries like IT. It took ten years to get it up and running. We are the first and only private training school in Ireland and probably in the whole of the UK. Our students leave with an MA qualification (Modern Apprenticeship) which is carried out through the NVQ system and includes crash repair, mechanical, light and heavy vehicle, parts distribution and, recently, engineering. It's a full-time four-year training and leaves them with an impressive, first-rate qualification that they can take anywhere in the world. Our students come to us straight from school, where they may not have thrived in such a strictly academic environment, usually with little confidence. We treat them as adults and show them respect. Their confidence and self-respect grow as they discover they are good at something, often incredibly so. It is wonderful to see them grow and develop.

I have only realised in the last few months what a big difference we've made to so many people's lives. We recently won the Top

Painter and Top Repairer awards which gained us a terrific amount of publicity. For years, I was always too busy setting up, directing and running the centre to talk to the individual apprentices we were training. It was only when I took a step back from being so completely driven that I realised the impact it's having. Since doing that, I am so much more aware of them and they love talking to me. I am always welcome in their garage!

I give every credit to the brilliant people around me who run the Centre. They are the ones making it all happen and putting their hearts into what they do and building the kids up. They do an incredible job. The buzz I get from seeing a shy, spotty, 16-year-old grow into a confident young man of 20 with valuable skills to begin life with is incredible. It doesn't compare to simply making more money. One of our graduates, Andrew Blair, has just won the UK Skills Award in vehicle body repair and will go on to represent the UK and Ireland at the WorldSkills Olympics in Helsinki, competing with crash repair apprentices from all over the world. Isn't that incredible – the best in the country and possibly the world? He'll definitely come away with a medal, and he's good enough to win. One of the best days of the year for me is our annual Graduation Day, when young men who have almost grown up with us receive their qualification. To see them leave equipped with a respected award and walk straight into a well-paid job with terrific prospects is brilliant. The job satisfaction I get then is just amazing. No balance sheet could give you that feeling, however healthy!

My driving force is no longer money. I'm now seeking to offer something charitable to people that will have an important impact and won't be solely commercial. I am ready to move on to something else, maybe somewhere else. We all have great skills and so, put together, we can make life much more worthwhile.

* * *

On 30 May 2005 Pamela called me to give me the news that Andrew Blair had won the Gold Medal in Autobody Repair at the WorldSkills Olympics in Helsinki! Looking at her sitting in the smart hotel in Dublin where we had arranged to meet, dressed in a quietly expensive outfit, she looked no different from all the other off-duty business types dotted around the place that Saturday morning. Her latest model Mercedes sports car had been safely valet-parked and we sat down to our fine coffee. Everything about her reeked of ease, comfort, success and affluence. She was everything you'd expect from a smart, award-winning businesswoman. I could easily have limited our conversation to her money-making tips or how she had transformed a small business into a much bigger one. But that would have been to miss a far more interesting story – of how and why she had set up a remarkable experiment to train unemployed youngsters to have practical skills that would last them for life. As you might expect, Pamela was keen to emphasise that it is the brilliant team at Blackwater House that is really responsible for the success of it all. They do the work. They have the expertise. Sure. But there's no escaping the fact that if she hadn't been big enough to want to set the whole thing up in the first place, there wouldn't be a Blackwater House.

I love what Pamela has done. Using her formidable drive, perseverance and sheer chutzpah, she has put a brilliant venture in place to help young people help themselves.

More to Life than Money

Money is indispensable in our world, but it doesn't buy everything. Like Pamela Morgan, many others are rethinking the value of money and the importance of fulfilment. In the UK there is a distinct trend for older, and affluent, workers to abandon their careers to retrain as teachers, taking the average age of trainees to 30. One typical example is Nick Hamlyn who was a £100,000-a-year banker and has retrained as a French teacher – on around £30,000. Nick, who is 43, says that his new career presents him with greater challenges and rewards than his old life ever did. He said, 'The money is not as good as in banking, but I never enjoyed banking very much . . . in your thirties you begin to realise that your life is no longer all in front of you.'

We're undergoing a revolution in the way we think about success. Money just doesn't have the status that it used to have, and a high-flying job means nothing if it costs you your health, marriage and family happiness. We no longer assume that a large house, big car and expensive holidays spell success. We're more likely to look beyond them for the all-too-familiar side-effects of poor health, dissatisfaction, divorce and troubled teenagers! The modern definition of a dream life is to have a fulfilling career, good health, a happy family life, hobbies and close friends. Recent surveys have been pointing out that men as young as 25 are having a mid-life crisis. Not necessarily. As I see it, young people are beginning to question the sort of life they want and looking aghast at some of the options! They are having to juggle with the dilemma of making money and having a life at the same time. Young people are less likely to be happy to comply with the demands of an all-consuming career if it requires such a colossal compromise on everything else in their life. That's not a crisis – that's a fascinating conversation.

If we're looking for a life with plenty of real crisis in it, we need look no further than my next case study. John Bird, founder of *The Big Issue* magazine, has some controversial ideas on generosity. Homeless himself in his early twenties, he set up a magazine for homeless people to sell to earn money. *The Big Issue* is a publishing phenomenon, sold on the streets of virtually every major city in the world. John stirred a national debate when he condemned the type of generosity that he feels ruins people rather than cushioning them. His 'constructive generosity' does not include giving money to beggars. Is there such a thing as too much generosity, or the wrong type of generosity?

John Bird

Paying unemployment benefit indefinitely and introducing the idea that it was wrong to chase up recipients to make sure they were looking for work has had terrible consequences for society. By changing the intrinsic purpose of the welfare state, we turned people into drones, dependent on the taxpayer. We took dignity and crushed it. We replaced it with handouts and undermined any sense of responsibility. The original architects of the welfare system would be horrified at the way it has mushroomed into a multimillion-pound bonanza for those who are unwilling to work but still believe the state owes them a living. The social experiment of the welfare state has backfired. The amazing state of affairs where people don't have to work for a living turns people into perennial children.

Men and women who are perfectly healthy should be made to take some form of employment. By relating work to benefit we get people up in the morning rather than letting them spend their time watching daytime TV. Recognition that you can't be supported without making a contribution is paramount. Getting people out of their dependency is the biggest contribution we can make to their wellbeing. The culture of handouts without work condemns the underclass to a lifetime in the ghetto.

I come from a very violent, antisocial background. My parents' frequent failure to pay the rent meant that at one point we were living in a boxroom in my grandmother's roof. I became really troubled and ended up in borstal for fraud. I hated everyone. I didn't know anyone who had any honour and that included my own family. I chose to become a runaway, jumping bail and travelling to Paris, Edinburgh and Aberdeen. For me it was an opportunity not to be pursued, bullied and beaten up. But once I'd got my record straight and become legitimate, I was never homeless again. I somehow got to go to art school but ended up getting a girl pregnant, marrying her and going off the rails again. My thieving and fighting went on into my mid–late twenties until I got involved in revolutionary politics. The Marxist global view knocked the racist, chauvinistic small-mindedness out of me. It was a real transformation. I remarried and became a father again. Mind you, I ended up getting kicked out of the movement for being a so-called 'anti-class thug'! I realised they were just a bunch of idealists. After a few jobs in printing, I set up on my own and became quite an excellent printer. My wife bought a house with sheds that we converted into my print shop in 1978. It was an instant success because I became incredibly passionate about what I did. The problem was I was so enthusiastic about turning out work that I neglected collecting the money. In the end I was owed an enormous amount but was too busy to chase it up.

I had been generous with others but not generous with myself. I was a social upholsterer, always addressing other people's problems and money worries. My cash flow suffered as a result. Some people misinterpret kindness. It was a great education in how to run a business. So, I told people what I could do for them, what I had done for them and then said, 'Now pay up.' I learnt not to be idealistic. A generous practical person is worth a hundred generous idealists. I became that one person who held on to my generosity but just tweaked it a little bit. I didn't become mean and cynical.

Years ago, Gordon Roddick, who started The Body Shop with his wife Anita, was in New York and bought a copy of Street News, *which was being sold by the homeless on the streets of Manhattan. The idea was that the public paid $1 and the vendor* *received 80 cents of that. Gordon got The Body Shop Foundation to do a feasibility study and involved all the big charities at the time like Shelter, Centrepoint, and Crisis at Christmas. But they came to the conclusion that it couldn't work in the UK and felt it would be exploiting the homeless! I'd met Gordon in 1967 in a pub in Edinburgh. I was 21 and on the run from the police. He was an ex-agricultural student and he'd just met Anita a couple of weeks before. We were both writing poetry at the time.*

Gordon was the first person I ever met who took me seriously. He listened to my crap poems and I loved the guy. Around 1987 he told me about his experience in New York. I was anti the dependency culture created by charities but I agreed to do a feasibility study on setting up a magazine that the homeless would sell. I was very impressed by the response to the idea from the Metropolitan Police and the homeless themselves. I said £30,000 was what was needed to finance it from conception to profit. After nine months, Gordon told me he had already given me £300,000 – but what's a nought amongst mates! In actual fact it took about £1.5 million to get us into profit. Gordon always says half of that was a waste of money but he doesn't know which half! I got together a non-professional team of friends and family and then we addressed ourselves to the homeless.

They had to buy the paper for 10p and sell it for 50p. They were so angry because they were used to handouts. They wanted to know why they were not getting it for nothing. It proved to be a big problem and created loads of fights. We were robbed – they'd break into the van and steal the magazines. We gave them twenty free papers to start them off and said if you want more, you have to pay 10p. It was hard-nosed and we fell out with a lot of the homeless organisations who felt it was exploitation. But we were bringing the homeless into the market-place. We got a lot of grief from the public as well, who wanted to give them £5 and keep them dependent.

We were acting in a mature way – solving the problem

without the handouts. Ten years ago we started an organisation called the International Network of Street Papers. The Big Issue *is now sold on every continent around the world with the exception of Antarctica. Last year we moved into Japan, for example, and it is a rip-roaring success. We are looking at places like Palestine and Iraq. This method lets the people become part of the transformation. I'm writing a book called* The Evils of Idealism, *about the fatal combination of wishful thinking and best intentions. One of the lessons of my life is that we have been screwed up as much by people trying to be nice and kind and generous as we have by naked exploitation. Misplaced institutionalised generosity from middle-class do-gooders is only perpetrating social injustice. The worst thing you can do for beggars is to give them money. It's not actually helping their mental or physical wellbeing. You end up giving money to people on the streets and unwittingly killing them. Forty to fifty per cent of those homeless people I work with are affected by mental health problems. We have to show them how to achieve success in easy steps. We need to find the ingredient that enables people to get their lives in gear, to aspire and be hopeful. In the right circumstances, given the right support, the mentally ill can get there but not on their own. In fact, I don't know anybody who has ever got anywhere on their own. I came from nothing; for years I had no role models, no love, no encouragement. I did make it in the end but had a series of mental breakdowns and became a very horrible person en route and would not recommend that to anyone. We all need a strong person who believes in us, and I know that without Gordon, I wouldn't have achieved what I have.*

But, you know, we have to get it wrong in order to get it right sometimes. The financial safety net offered now has no give in it and is like concrete. People are being drip-fed just enough to stay alive but are left with a strong sense of their own inferiority. We have to use our generosity constructively and not set people up to fail.

Constructive Generosity

John's 'tough love' approach, or 'constructive generosity' as he calls it, makes sense to me. If you remove people's need to exercise personal responsibility for themselves, where's the incentive to push themselves to make life work? A few years ago I used to coach people on a well-known daytime television programme. Their complaints ranged from obesity to lethargy to depression to agoraphobia. More often, they were either unemployed or receiving sickness benefits. Usually, when I inquired why they weren't working, their answer was, 'I can't afford to. I get more money from benefits than a job. I'd lose my allowances. It wouldn't pay me to work.' State generosity had stifled their creativity, inventiveness and – urgency.

I liked John immensely and I found his compassion genuine, thought-out and practical. He knows more than most what it feels like to be homeless and isolated: his opinion is informed with real, first-hand insight. He looks every one of his 59 years! I found him terrific company, funny, and a great raconteur; joking as we arranged to meet in his local Starbucks that it was a great place even though it was a 'bastion of imperialist capitalism'! Listening to him talk I could see that he is naturally generous and had clearly had to think deeply about how to use that largesse, for his benefit and others. I liked the fact that he hadn't given up on being generous after his generosity had nearly cost him his printing business all those years ago. He became a generous practical person rather than a generous idealist. Thankfully, he didn't opt for small-minded and cynical.

Stay Big

Coincidentally, I have recently had to rethink my own generosity after having 'adopted' a homeless beggar, bringing him into our home to give Jamie guitar lessons. Kevin stole thousands of pounds from us, disappearing with credit cards and money. When I finally tracked him down a week later to a filthy flat in east London, he was in a terrible state, barely able to talk, having spent the money on the heroin habit that I naïvely hadn't even noticed. My generosity had taken him perilously close to death. However, I have no intention of ending up mean and small-minded: I'm joining John to become a generous practical person instead of a generous idealist. In other words, I've learnt how generosity can actually backfire and end up helping someone stay helpless. In fact, you can make matters worse by unwittingly encouraging them to depend on you for their survival and removing their incentive to take responsibility for their own welfare, health and happiness. From now on, I will endeavour to help people *to help themselves*.

But in talking to John, I could also see how generosity often attracts the same back and draws people to you. I felt certain that if Gordon Roddick hadn't offered him *The Big Issue*, someone else would have offered him something else. Generosity is such an appealing characteristic that others find it immensely attractive. As I left Starbucks, I looked round to wave, but John was busy clearing our table, saving the staff the trouble. Now that's what I call generous!

From all the case studies in this chapter, one thing stands out and it's this: life is a whole lot more interesting and more rewarding with generosity at the centre of it. You are a bigger, more compelling and charismatic person when you have a bigger agenda in front of you. You're beyond the average person's remit of money and possessions. You're playing a bigger game, with more important considerations than your own comfort and security. You don't chase money, but it comes to you none the less. Adam, Chris, Pamela and John didn't focus on money. They focused on doing a great job. They all had a grand idea, a big scheme that inspired them. It was never about the money. It was about service, improving things and helping others. Adam wanted to be part of a company that made healthy food and was run along ethical lines; Chris wanted to do a great job and make his cafés terrific places to be; Pamela wanted to give young people the skills and tools to make their lives work; and John wanted to give the homeless a way of making their own living and getting back on their feet again. All of this adds up to a dynamic, exciting and sometimes dramatic life. It keeps you young and it probably keeps you slim as well!

Money is important, but it doesn't buy everything. It doesn't reach the parts that generosity reaches, in terms of the deep satisfaction you get from achieving something that benefits others. Even if your venture has to generate profit, go about it with a generous heart. In fact, all of the ventures featured here are commercial, but they are driven by the desire to provide a brilliant service in the first and final instance. Putting your life to good use doesn't require you to join a holy order. It just requires generosity in your everyday life.

Five Steps to be More Generous

1. Feel more generous. Fire up your inner levels of generosity by counting your blessings. Increase your satisfaction with life by keeping a gratitude journal. Write down three to five things from the mundane to the magnificent for which you are thankful, every day and every week.

2. Practise what you preach. If you run a business, make sure it's founded on twenty-first-century principles of fairness and generosity. Declare your ethics for all to see. Stand out from the competition and let people feel good about spending their pound, dollar and euro with you. It's not just what they're buying – but what they're buying into.

3. Do more than your shift at work. Don't be mean with your energy and efforts. Don't hold back, but do ensure that your generosity is reciprocated. Generosity isn't always its own reward. Be generous to yourself, too. No one likes a martyr!

4. Incorporate acts of generosity into your daily life. Buy fair-trade goods and enjoy the worthwhile buzz of knowing the farmers are getting a fair deal. Wear Edun jeans. Look great. Feel fabulous! Carry out regular and random acts of kindness. Have a bit of fun with it. Join the karma army of kindness and enjoy the solidarity.

5. Practise constructive generosity. Don't be a generous idealist: handouts don't work. But don't be cynical about generosity – it's a powerful tool. People need a hand-up rather than a handout to get back on their feet. Targeted generosity can transform the lives of others, and your own.

And **FINALLY . . .**

Now you know the 7 Rules of Success. All you have to do is follow them.

Apply them in your thinking and in your actions. Remember, you can choose your mindset. You can think like a winner. You can be passionate, fuelled by strong self-belief, a doer, a risk-taker, someone who perseveres, is inspiring and generous. You can inherit all these characteristics from the brilliant people in this book. Some you already possess; others you may want to enhance and develop.

Beyond your thinking is what you do. Above all, ensure that you're doing what you love. Don't do what you loathe and clock-watch. It would be unwise to assume that time is on your side, at any age. You are what you do. If you want to write, write. If you want to design, design. Whatever you want to do, do it. Then you're a person who does things, not a person who'll definitely do them when they've finished what they're doing now.

Be patient. Change takes time. Think productively, put the work in and you'll get results. Worst-case scenario, you take a few wrong turns en route. The big thing you can do wrong in life is waste time. The best way to fast-track to success is to get back-up. Email me, fiona@fionaharrold.com, and I'll find you a brilliant coach. Use our website and support to get yourself on track and keep yourself there. Put together your own Rules

Group of smart folk and motivate yourselves to follow the rules to your own success. You can find like-minded people on my site at www.fionaharrold.com or simply set up your own local group. Here are some guidelines to get you started:

- Keep your group small – no more than four people.
- Meet regularly, once a week or fortnight and commit to making the group a priority.
- Keep meetings short and dynamic. Agree the length before you start.
- Ensure total openness by signing a group confidentiality agreement.
- Work on one Rule per meeting. Choose a specific project and apply the Rules to it, one Rule per week.
- Ensure everyone in the group has the same allocated amount of time to discuss their project. Don't interrupt – give feedback at the end.
- Avoid giving advice. Instead, draw out solutions. Encourage, be generous and sensitive.
- Agree on a plan of action before moving on to the next person.

I salute you for having the get-up-and-go to have come this far. You've got ambition, drive and guts. You're brave. You don't shirk from the challenge of self-improvement and the responsibility of making your life truly successful. I admire you for that. I wish you every success until our paths cross.

Fiona Harrold
London, 2005